Station Hospital Saigon

LCDR Bobbi Hovis, NC, USN (Ret.)

Naval Institute Press
Annapolis, Maryland

STATION HOSPITAL SAIGON

A Navy Nurse in Vietnam, 1963–1964

Library of Congress Cataloging-in-Publication Data
Hovis, Bobbi.
  Station Hospital Saigon : a Navy nurse in Vietnam, 1963–1964 /
Bobbi Hovis.
     p.   cm.
  Includes bibliographical references and index.
  ISBN 1-55750-376-1
  1. Vietnamese Conflict, 1961–1975—Medical care. 2. Vietnamese Conflict,
1961–1975—Personal narratives, American. 3. Station Hospital Saigon (U.S.)
4. Hovis, Bobbi.   I. Title.
DS559.44.H68   1991   91-45414
959.704'37—dc20   CIP

Printed in the United States of America on acid-free paper ∞

9   8   7   6   5   4   3   2

First printing

Often, memories fade and diminish with the ongoing rush of time. But some events, people, and places are never really lost. It is possible, I found, to stimulate, retrieve, and even enhance memories—remembrances that fill this log. To all the Navy nurses who served at Station Hospital Saigon and to the rest of the staff, this collection of shared memories is dedicated.

Contents

Foreword

UPON MEETING the author, LCDR Bobbi Hovis, for the first time, you would immediately recognize her outstanding attribute—unbounded enthusiasm. It is contagious and revolves around all things pertaining to the Navy, with a particular focus on the Nurse Corps, the Naval Academy, and Navy football. Her avocation centers on sports, sailing, and a deep affection for one breed of dog, dachshunds. Bobbi becomes immersed in whatever she elects to do. Many of her contemporaries have eagerly awaited the final draft of her proposed manuscript, which documents her experiences in Saigon during the years 1963–64.

Bobbi retired from the Navy to the "Land of Pleasant Living and Unsurpassed Sailing"—the Chesapeake Bay, Annapolis, Maryland. For a time, at least, she was free to sail and to become the Naval Academy's number one fan.

Fortunately for us, while Bobbi placed her manuscript on hold for some years, *Station Hospital Saigon: A Navy Nurse in Vietnam, 1963–1964* has emerged. And what an adventure it is! It is a story of perseverance and courage, dedication and enthusiasm—qualities necessary to fulfill the mission of the Navy Medical Department, given the political climate in 1963. The concept of closing a dispensary and four days later opening a fully operational hospital ready to receive patients is mind-boggling under the best of circumstances. The miracle of transforming a dilapidated apartment building into a functioning medical treatment facility in ninety-six hours is overwhelming.

Only knowledgeable and determined medical department personnel could have made this seemingly impossible task a reality. In spite of the shortcomings of the physical plant, the Navy hospital known as

Duong Duong cared for combat casualties for two and a half years—until the facility was transferred to the Army in 1966. Navy health-care providers treated 6,000 inpatients and 130,000 outpatients while the hospital was under Navy command. The medical staff struggled with the shortage of personnel, supplies, and equipment—as well as with the difficulty of functioning in an inadequate facility. With ingenuity and a "can do" spirit, the personnel accepted each challenge as it arose and delivered outstanding patient care.

This is not only a story about a hospital. Bobbi writes about people involved in a war in Southeast Asia and creates a realistic picture for the reader. Her observational skills and in-depth recollection of people and circumstances make Saigon come alive and her friends and co-workers real. Her descriptions of sights, sounds, and odors bring the city to life. One feels the emotions of caring for combat casualties.

At the time that Bobbi was assigned to Saigon (1963–64), she was a seasoned and experienced Nurse Corps officer. During her many tours in naval hospitals in the United States and overseas, she developed a broad background of clinical expertise. In addition, Bobbi was a member of the elite group of flight nurses who flew medevac missions during the Korean War.

Station Hospital Saigon is most important to the history of military women. There is a scarcity of literature written by women veterans concerning their experiences in war. A walk through a bookstore will reveal a significant number of books available on the male war experience, while similar literature on women is almost nonexistent. One cannot fault the male military establishment for this disparity. Culturally, our nation has denied the role women play in war; regrettably, women have acquiesced.

Men, depicted as warriors and honored as such, write about war. Women, the "nonwarriors," have traditionally remained silent; excluded from the body of war literature, their stories mostly go untold. The lack of written documentation concerning women's experiences in war, however, fails to obliterate them from the memories of those with whom they served. Obviously, Lieutenant Commander Hovis's book is important to military women past and present, nurses, and non-nurses. But interest should expand to a much broader audience. This account reflects situations and people having historical significance in the total picture of the Vietnam experience. I think many men will gain a different perspective by viewing war through a woman's eyes. Vice Adm. Ross T. McIntyre, surgeon general of the Navy during World War II, wrote that "Navy Nurses are women of action, rather than words: their honors, successes and deeds have gone unheralded." Bobbi Hovis changes that well-meaning stereotype. She melds actions with words to give us an accurate, dynamic, stirring account of a Navy nurse's Vietnam experience.

—RADM Frances Shea Buckley, NC, USN (Ret.)
former Director, Navy Nurse Corps

Acknowledgments

I WISH TO EXPRESS my deepest appreciation and thanks to the following people—all very special friends. Without their assistance and support this memoir would have stayed packed away in the depths of my old sea chest.

Lil Wray, for the early encouragement that led to the plotting of the course.

Karen and Joe DiRenzo, for clearing the decks for action.

Tweedie Searcy, for making me stay the course.

Debby Regimenti, for helping me transform the rough log, envisioning a smooth one, and encouraging me to find that which I feared was lost.

Mike Regimenti, Chief Engineer, who stood computer and printer watch and kept the machinery oiled and running at full bore.

Fran Shea Buckley, who gave much valued advice, knowledge, and support throughout this mission.

Mark Gatlin and all the other staff members at the Naval Institute Press for having faith that this final log was possible.

And Elsa van Bergen, for making the final log Bristol fashion.

The Creeds

Florence Nightingale Pledge

(Stated by all nurses who successfully complete a six-month probationary period. This pledge is taken during the capping ceremony.)

I solemnly pledge to myself in the presence of this assembly that I will practice my profession in honesty and sincerity. I will act as a patient advocate and devote myself to the welfare of those committed to my care. I will aid the physician with whom I share a mutual concern for my patient's best interests. I will uphold the rights of the patients and hold all their personal matters in confidence. I will elevate the standards of my profession and help others in all facets of life: the joy of birth, the pain and suffering of illness and the grief of death.

(Revised in 1980)

Oath of Office

(This oath is taken by all officers who enter naval service.)

I [name] having been appointed [rank] in the U.S. Navy under the conditions indicated in this document, do accept such appointment and do solemnly swear (or affirm) that I will support and defend the Constitution of the United States against all enemies, foreign and domestic, that I will bear true faith and allegiance to the same; that I take this obligation freely, without any mental reservation or purpose of evasion; and that I will well and faithfully discharge the duties of the office on which I am about to enter, so help me God.

Flight Nurse's Creed

I will summon every resource to prevent the triumph of death over life. I will stand guard over the medicines and equipment entrusted to my care and insure their proper use. I will be untiring in the performances of my duties and I will remember that, upon my disposition and spirit, will in large measure depend the morale of my patients. I will be faithful to my training and to the wisdom handed down to me by those who have gone before us. I have taken a nurse's oath, reverent in man's mind because of the spirit and work of its creator, Florence Nightingale. She, I remember, was called the "lady with the lamp." It is now my privilege to lift this lamp of hope and faith and courage in my profession to heights not known by her in her time. Together with the help of flight surgeons and surgical technicians, I can set the very skies ablaze with life and promise for the sick, injured and wounded who are my sacred charges. This I will do, I will not falter in war or in peace.

Station Hospital Saigon

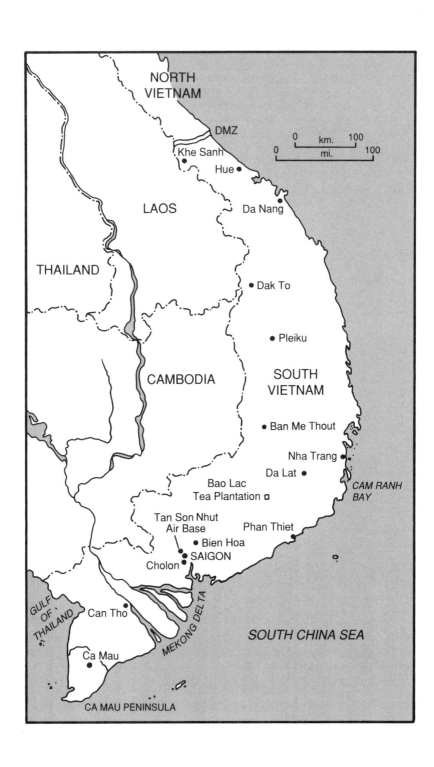

Prologue to Vietnam

IN ORDER TO EQUALIZE the areas of responsibility taken on by the branches of the military, the Department of Defense in the early 1960s divided the globe into regions. By March 1962, the three branches of the armed forces, and with them their medical departments, were each assigned certain territories. The area from Bien Hoa, twenty miles north of Saigon, to the tip of the Ca Mau Peninsula in the Mekong Delta came under the jurisdiction of the Department of the Navy. Included therein was the city of Saigon, the capital of South Vietnam.

The war in Vietnam was escalating. As one source summarized the buildup: "In December of 1961, [President John F. Kennedy] sent in three hundred helicopter pilots. Within a few months, the American military support group had increased to four thousand people. By 1963, the United States was a real military force in Vietnam. . . ."* Another history of the time reports that "within two years of Kennedy's taking of office some 15,000 members of the American military forces were in Vietnam."†

It became apparent to the Navy's Bureau of Medicine and Surgery that several members of the Navy Nurse Corps would be needed in Saigon for the purpose of providing medical support to the American community. Previously, this responsibility for both American military and civilian personnel had been assumed by the American embassy. But as increasing numbers of American troops and civilians poured into South Vietnam, the subsequent rise in combat casualties, the increase in Viet Cong terrorist victims, and the dangerous variety of tropical dis-

*Denis J. Hauptley, *In Vietnam* (New York: Atheneum, 1985), 82–83.
†Don Lawson, *An Album of the Vietnam War* (New York: Franklin Watts, 1986), 14.

eases all indicated the need for bigger and better hospital facilities. As a result of this expansion, more Navy nurses were required there.

In February 1963, two Navy nurses were ordered to the seventeen-bed American Dispensary in Saigon. Shortly thereafter, five more of us were on the way to Saigon, a city in continual crisis, and to new challenges in the practice of our profession. The tour of duty was one year; the receipt of orders to South Vietnam promised our privileged group twelve months of unparalleled adventure. Our course had been set. We were sailors embarking on an uncertain voyage in seas that were as inviting, even compelling, and strangely beautiful as they were chaotic. This voyage would mark the beginning of another colorful and unique chapter in the illustrious history of the Navy Nurse Corps. It would also lead me to the high point of my career.

The foundation for the Corps was laid as far back as 1811, when a Navy surgeon, Dr. William Barton, was appointed by the Secretary of the Navy to make recommendations for managing hospitals and institutions. Interestingly, his recommendation to include nurses in the Navy's hospital planning preceded by nine years the birth of Florence Nightingale, who would become the symbol of nursing.

During the Civil War, in 1862, a confiscated Confederate steamer, *Red Rover,* was converted into a floating hospital—making it our first U.S. Navy hospital ship. Four nurses—Catholic nuns and Sisters of Holy Cross—volunteered to administer nursing care aboard, and as such they became the first female nurses with shipboard duties. It is believed that these remarkable women, the predecessors of the official Navy Nurse Corps, continued to serve aboard the *Red Rover* until that ship's services were discontinued in 1865. At that point, it was male sailors, acting as corpsmen, who provided, almost exclusively, the nursing care for the Navy.

Nurses again saw wartime duty in service to the Navy during the Spanish-American War. A group of trained nurses, neither enlisted nor enrolled nor certain that they would be paid, were assigned to the Naval Hospital, Norfolk, Virginia, in 1898. However, the golden opportunity to create a skilled and dedicated Navy Nurse Corps slipped away. Despite repeated campaigns to win congressional approval for a Corps, such approval was not forthcoming until 13 May 1908.

Because women were not admitted to the Navy until World War I—as yeomanettes—a status known as relative rank was created to accommodate female nurses as noncommissioned personnel. Although denied rank and stripes, they received pay commensurate with, or related to that of, male Navy staff. (In 1947, the Navy Nurse Corps achieved its present status, with full rank and pay, as a separate Corps under the Bureau of Medicine and Surgery.)

In August 1908, twenty women achieved the status of relative rank and reported to the Naval Hospital (now Bethesda Naval Hospital) in Washington, D.C. Later known as the Sacred Twenty, these women were true hybrids. Although civilians, they assumed special status because their pay and some of their benefits were assumed by the Navy and because they were subject to naval disciplinary measures.

Of course today's Navy is different. Since 1976, women have been admitted to the U.S. Naval Academy. With training for combat billets still limited, women continue to serve the Navy in a broad range of noncombat disciplines—as, for example, intelligence officers, oceanographic engineers, computer specialists, and aviators. There exists an irony in the admission of women to the Naval Academy. As a traditional military school, the academy educates midshipmen in preparation for combat roles. Women, however, are excluded by law from assuming those roles, though the laws may change. Interestingly, nursing is one aspect of a Navy career that cannot be pursued at the U.S. Naval Academy.

At the beginning of World War I, the Navy had no hospitals in Europe. However, several Navy nurses were released for temporary duty to serve with the Red Cross in France, and a few were temporarily assigned duty with Army field units in that country. By 1917, Navy base hospitals were organized in France, Ireland, Scotland, and England.

Wartime Navy Nurse Corps involvement resumed in December 1941, when the U.S. possession Guam was captured by Japanese invaders. Five Navy nurses were included among the prisoners of war. They were interned in a military prison in Japan, repatriated in August 1942, and returned to the United States aboard the Swedish exchange ship *Gripsholm*.

Navy nursing had been established in the hospital, the field, and aboard ship by late 1943. One other significant aspect of Navy, as opposed to civilian, nursing was addressed in December of that year. Flight nursing was introduced into the Corps when two Navy nurses were ordered to the Army's Bowman Field in San Antonio, Texas; there they received training in medical air evacuation of the wounded. Following graduation they proceeded to Rio de Janeiro, where they acted as advisers to the Brazilian Air Force. This was a first. As advisers, these women were responsible for helping to organize a training program in air evacuation (airevac, or, as it is now generally known, medevac) procedures.

The Navy's first school for flight nursing was established in December 1944 at the Naval Air Station, Alameda, California. In February 1945, graduates of the program staged on Guam and stood by to fly medevac missions out of Iwo Jima and Okinawa. One of them was the late Jane Kendeigh, the first woman to arrive on Iwo Jima—just hours following the Japanese surrender of the island.

During World War II, the Corps expanded to include more than eleven thousand members. These nurses were assigned to 40 naval hospitals, 176 dispensaries, and 6 hospital corps schools within the continental United States. And at overseas land bases in the Aleutian Islands, Alaska, Australia, the Admiralty Islands, Africa, Bermuda, Cuba, the Canal Zone, England, Hawaii, Italy, the Mariana Islands, New Caledonia, New Hebrides, New Zealand, Newfoundland, Puerto Rico, the Russell Islands, the Solomon Islands, and Trinidad, Navy nurses could be found skillfully administering to sick and wounded servicemen.

In forward areas of sea battle, Navy nurses carried out their duties aboard twelve hospital ships. Many nurses were sent to far and remote foreign shores staffing base, fleet, and mobile naval hospitals. In the New Hebrides, site of one of these units, Navy nurses were the first American women the natives had ever seen.

With the end of the war, during 1945–47, massive demobilization ensued. The Navy Nurse Corps was reduced to fewer than a thousand members. It was during this period, on 16 October 1947, that I joined the Corps.

The Navy became my life. I had been born in Girard, Ohio, in 1925 and soon moved with my family to Edinboro, Pennsylvania. Raised on the shores of Lake Edinboro, I developed a love of sailing and became totally water oriented. Several in my family served in the Navy on submarine tenders and as medical doctors. These were some of the reasons that by the time of the attack on Pearl Harbor, 7 December 1941, I had decided to pursue a career in Navy nursing. I was sixteen years old.

My nurse's training at the Western Pennsylvania Hospital in Pittsburgh followed graduation from Edinboro High School. In 1947, I received my appointment as an ensign in the Navy Nurse Corps, undergoing indoctrination training at the U.S. Naval Air Station, Naval Hospital, Jacksonville, Florida. It was the farthest from my home in Edinboro that

I had ever traveled. And it was the door to a wondrous world of experiences—both personally and professionally.

In 1950, I completed my flight-nurse training at the Air University, School of Aviation Medicine at Gunter Air Force Base, Montgomery, Alabama. On 25 June of that year the North Korean army crossed the 38th parallel, the line of demarcation between North and South Korea. Thus began the "police action" that became the Korean War. I was on night duty at the Naval Hospital, Key West, Florida. The radio was playing in the OD's (officer of the day's) office when the announcement came.

Recalling it now, forty years later, I can still recapture in my memory the charge of excitement that shot through me. Within hours the Navy Nurse Corps, its ranks recently diminished, suddenly exploded with the immediate call-up of reserves. The hospital ship USS *Consolation,* along with her nursing crew, arrived off Korean waters in July 1950. She was soon joined by the USS *Repose* and the USS *Haven.* Together, these hospital ships provided invaluable medical support to the combat units.

Tragedy struck almost immediately. Steaming out of port on her shakedown cruise, the hospital ship *Benevolence* collided with a merchant vessel in San Francisco Bay on 25 August, capsized, and sank. All hands were rescued, but sadly one of the nurses died shortly after as a result of exposure to the icy waters.

In the Pacific Ocean, more than four thousand miles from San Francisco Bay, another tragedy unfolded just one month later. A Navy transport aircraft taking off from Kwajalein, Marshall Islands, crashed into the sea a short distance from the runway. All aboard perished, including eleven Navy nurses. These nurses, en route to Yokosuka, Japan, would have seen Korean War action. Their deaths impressed upon their fellow nurses that the hazards of war knew no sexual boundaries. We were all at risk.

Three months later, I was assigned to the Korean airlift. While flying over San Francisco Bay, I was able to observe below the shimmering white hull of the *Benevolence,* her three red crosses still visible. She was never salvaged for repair. As the sight of her faded, I was subdued. There would no doubt be excitement, but there would also be sacrifice.

As in World War II, Navy nurses served with distinction by flying around-the-clock medevac missions over the far reaches of the ocean to bring home casualties. I was immensely proud to be part of this huge air evacuation system. During the Korean War, peak strength of the Corps reached almost 3,300 officers. With the release of recalled reserves, the numbers dropped to the 2,400 level, but today there are 5,300 active-duty nurses, an increase dictated by the needs of the naval service. Between the conflicts in Korea and Vietnam, the Navy Nurse Corps saw many changes. There were increased opportunities for its members to further their education and consequently to advance in rank. New hospital facilities were established in such far-flung places as Nice, France; Taiwan; Rota, Spain; Keflavik, Iceland; Roosevelt Roads, Puerto Rico; Sigonella, Sicily; and Perth, Australia; there was also a billet for a Navy nurse in the White House in Washington, D.C. And in September 1958 the Corps took another step into the modern age. A four-month course in nuclear medicine was established at the Department of Nuclear Medicine in the Naval Medical School at the National Naval Medical Center, Bethesda, Maryland. Following course completion, nurses were assigned to the naval hospitals where radioisotope laboratories had been established.

The first male nurse entered the Corps on 25 August 1965. Since his admission, the ranks of male nurses have increased. Like their female counterparts, men are assigned to facilities all over the world; male or female, Navy nurses perform similar tasks.

The Corps's wartime history had been full of challenges and achievements—and often danger. Yet few of those past experiences quite equaled those awaiting us in Vietnam. There, battle lines were obscure. The concept of guerrilla warfare, with the enemy wearing no military uniform and thus being impossible to differentiate from the civilian population, presented unique dangers—and a situation in which we treated more victims of Viet Cong terrorist attacks than of conventional battlefield wounds during my time in Vietnam. The word *terrorism* has taken on a somewhat special connotation in recent years, but the type of violent activity practiced by the Viet Cong, and their objects of attack—civilians, off-duty military, restaurants, and hospitals—made it the only word for what we observed in 1963 and 1964. Indeed, this urban terrorism stemmed from a real campaign of terror begun in 1959 by Viet Cong guerrillas, who aimed to destroy the rural dwellers' confidence in the South Vietnamese government by eliminating such citizens as officials, civil workers, and teachers.[*]

We who were among the first nurses ordered to serve in this uncommon conflict were promised the opportunity of adding some compel-

*Department of Defense, *A Pocket Guide to Viet-Nam* (Washington, D.C.: U.S. Government Printing Office, 1962), 23.

ling pages to the distinguished log of the Navy Nurse Corps. What follows is my account, based on letters written home during the months I served in Saigon and preserved by family and friends. Those letters included witness to key events that helped turn American "assistance" and "action" into war. It is my hope that these memoirs serve the collective remembrances of my fellow nurses with whom I shared that time.

ONE
Orders to Saigon

4 AUGUST 1963
FROM: CHIEF OF NAVAL PERSONNEL
TO: COMMANDING OFFICER, U.S. NAVAL HOSPITAL, QUANTICO,
VIRGINIA
INFO: COMMANDANT TWELFTH NAVAL DISTRICT
UNCLASSIFIED
BUPERS ORDERS NUMBER 021091
LCDR VILA J. HOVIS, NURSE CORPS, 509173/2900 HEREBY DETACHED.
PROCEED SUCH TRANSPORTATION COMTWELVE DESIGNATES TO SAI-
GON, REPUBLIC OF VIETNAM. ARRIVE REPORT TO HEDSUPPACT FOR
DUTY. DELAY REPORTING PORT OF ENTRY BY 10 SEPTEMBER. GOVERN-
MENT TRANSPORTATION AUTHORIZED. BAGGAGE BY AIR 165 LBS
AUTHORIZED. IMMUNIZATIONS REQUIRED. PRIOR DETACHMENT
COMMAND DELIVERING ORDERS SHALL INSURE THAT SHE IS ORI-
ENTED IN CODE OF CONDUCT FOR MEMBERS OF THE ARMED FORCES
AND DANGERS OF COMMUNISM.

THE FOURTH OF AUGUST 1963 fell on a Saturday. I was preparing to spend an afternoon sailing on the Potomac River when the phone rang. It was the duty officer at the hospital asking me to come right over. I wasted no time getting there, and when I arrived I was handed dispatch orders. Bristling only at the sight of my given name—I much prefer Bobbi—I saw that I was going to Vietnam. Thirteen years earlier I had received a similar set of orders assigning me to duty as a flight nurse attached to the Korean airlift. For the second time in my career I was going to participate in a war.

Orders to Saigon

I was thirty-eight years old and a senior Navy nurse with sixteen years' experience. I had been assigned to the Naval Station Hospital at Quantico Marine Base, Quantico, Virginia, in December 1960. Ordinarily my current tour of duty might have continued another year or longer. But the times were exceptional.

And the orders weren't unexpected. During the summer, my good friend and fellow nurse, Lt. Comdr. Owedia (Tweedie) Searcy was invited by the Navy Nurse Corps Detail Officer, Capt. Romaine Mentzer, to meet with her at the Navy Bureau of Medicine and Surgery in Washington, D.C. Tweedie and Captain Mentzer discussed an upcoming tour of duty in Saigon and the establishment of a naval station hospital there. Tweedie knew that I wanted an assignment in Vietnam. On my behalf she volunteered me for duty. At the conclusion of the interview, Captain Mentzer told Tweedie that I, too, could most likely expect orders to Saigon.

As a nurse anesthetist, Tweedie would head the Anesthesia Department and the Emergency, Operating, and Central Supply rooms at the new hospital. A petite blonde Texan, she had at one time earned the nickname Stormy, but this represented an oxymoron: far from wreaking havoc, Tweedie could restore order and keep an operating room schedule moving crisply. There was never any anchor dragging when Tweedie was on duty. My specialty was in the surgical area and in the surgical and orthopedic wards; at the new facility I would be working in the Operating and Recovery rooms and in the Intensive Care Unit.

Since our orders were dispatch rather than routine we had only twenty-four hours to detach from Quantico on 6 August, with Sunday, 5 August, as an extra day, since detachments were not effected on Sundays. Following detachment I had thirty days' leave. Tweedie and I had to rent out the house we shared, store the furnishings, and pack quickly. In addition there were will preparations, immunizations, overseas physical and dental exams. One day we received a letter from Comdr. Florence Alwyn, a senior Navy nurse already stationed at the American Dispensary in Saigon. Her letter was chock-full of advice and helpful hints such as bringing shoes one size larger than normal: Flo had discovered that feet swelled in the heat and humidity of Vietnam.

Because there was no Navy anesthetist in Saigon, Tweedie decided to pack a footlocker with some equipment and drugs essential to the administration of anesthesia. Should they be needed, it would be in a hurry, and these items would have to be at her fingertips. A life might depend on it. As we would see, several lives were indeed saved because of her foresight.

We prepared in other ways. I studied the information that had come with my orders. The official literature included a book, *The Dangers of Communism,* and a helpful and interesting booklet, *A Pocket Guide to Viet-Nam,* which gave a brief history of Vietnam as well as facts concerning customs, culture, and language. A number of customs, I read, derive from elaborate sets of religious beliefs. While the Vietnamese are often warm, helpful, and cooperative, they most highly value respect for privacy, the honor of family, and behavior in accordance with traditional beliefs. For example, for many, parts of the human body are thought to possess varying degrees of significance or worthiness, and therefore patting someone on the head might be considered a serious insult.* Even techniques of greeting and beckoning were part of a new language we would need to learn.

As the leave time passed, Tweedie and I made brief trips to visit both of our families. At my parents' home in Edinboro, I parted with Snoopy, my dachshund puppy. She adapted to her new environment with enthusiasm, and my parents were delighted with their foster pup. Frequent progress reports were promised. The next time I would see her she would be full grown.

I experienced a bittersweet mixture of emotions. The reality of my Saigon assignment was drawing nearer. I was only slightly aware of an inner process that was helping me shift emotionally from a perspective of family, friends, anxieties, and assurances to one of duty and my job as a Navy nurse. This subtle shift in mindset served me as "slipping the mooring lines"—the break with those left behind—serves the sailor. A metamorphosis was under way as I began to ease those ties and look ahead to an uncertain and rapidly approaching future.

We arrived in San Francisco on 10 September, spending a couple of days sightseeing, shopping, and visiting with Navy friends. At the Bachelor Officers' Quarters (BOQ) at Treasure Island Naval Base, I met a South Vietnamese navy supply corps officer who was receiving specialized training at the Naval Supply School, training that was not available in South Vietnam. In response to my expressions of curiosity about our Navy's role in Vietnam and about the efforts of the South Vietnamese, the lieutenant commander began to speak at length about his homeland. His opinion was that from a military perspective South Vietnam

*Department of Defense, *A Pocket Guide to Viet-Nam* (Washington, D.C.: U.S. Government Printing Office, 1962), 63.

was disorganized. On top of that, unrest, primarily caused by conflicts between Catholics and Buddhists, had forced the imposition of martial law. Saigon would be an exciting assignment, he assured us.

The terminal at Travis Air Force Base was jammed when we arrived on 12 September. Still we were able to pick out the summer-blue Dacron uniforms that identified the other Navy nurses who had received dispatch orders to Vietnam. It was a special group: two lieutenant commanders and three lieutenants were embarking to join Flo Alwyn and Penny Kauffman, who were already attached to the American Dispensary in Saigon.

We located Elaine King, tall and dark-haired, first. As she greeted us I noticed her New England accent. Her warm manner made me immediately comfortable, and I felt as though I had known her for a long time. Jan Barcott arrived with her aunt. She seemed quiet—a private, introspective person. I sensed that she had some qualms about setting off for Vietnam—though she kept them to herself. The last to arrive was Carleda Lorberg. I knew Carleda, a bubbly dynamo, from my days at Oakland Naval Hospital. She was at that time a new ensign, scatterbrained, perpetually late—a real handful. I had been her supervisor then and as I looked at her approaching I discovered I had retained some sense of responsibility for Carleda. I hoped that she had grown up in the five years since Oakland.

It wasn't long before our flight was called; we would be boarding in twenty minutes. I headed for the telephones and called my parents. Snoopy, I learned, had an inflamed paw and was scheduled to visit the vet. It may seem extraordinary to some, but that bit of news dampened my spirits, tempered a bit the slipping of the mooring lines. Pets have always been an important part of my life, and I care for all animals deeply.

We boarded a 707C World Airways jetliner and blocked out on time at 1700 hours. Minutes later the 707 crossed the coastline and headed out over the darkening Pacific Ocean. I had mixed feelings as the aircraft circled and climbed on its way to, in the words of Associated Press reporter Hugh Mulligan, "a strange land, a land of paradoxes and contrasts; the East at its most inscrutable. Also at its most gracious and exciting." Mulligan omitted one very significant word, however. Vietnam was also *dangerous*.

Dawn was breaking as our 707 left the South China Sea behind and descended over the troubled but beautiful country of South Vietnam. With the rising of the sun, the land below became bathed in rays of molten gold. Canals crisscrossed the land mass, and other waterways appeared as silver threads winding in and around rich green rice paddies. Rubber plantations produced dark green patches superimposed on the lighter greens, browns, golds, and silvers. I thought I was looking down on a fine, intricate tapestry. We continued to descend. The waterways now became more distinct. Thatched huts were nestled in copses of bamboo trees and coconut palms. Water buffalo were enjoying the morning's first wallowing.

The aircraft touched down and we taxied to a stop. We were in South Vietnam. I couldn't have guessed that we were about to participate in what would ultimately become the tragedy of a lost cause.

TWO

Rooms with a View

FRIDAY THE THIRTEENTH had been lost in crossing the international date line. Twenty-three hours had elapsed since departure from Travis, and we were exhausted. As we stepped down from the aircraft at Tan Son Nhut Air Base, the heat hit us with the force of a blast furnace. In our state we found the heat and the accompanying humidity enervating, but all around us the air base bustled with activity. Along the runways, C-123s, the workhorses of Vietnam-era aircraft, turned up engines in preparation for an early morning airlift or a paratroop drop. A company of soldiers from the Army of the Republic of Vietnam (ARVN), attired in full battle dress—bandoliers of ammunition, grenades hanging from webbing, full backpacks, radio, and weapons—was boarding. Farther down the flight line, armed helicopters loaded other troops.

We deplaned and were escorted by the briefing officer to a sparsely furnished hut in which there were no fans or windows. The officer instructed us on the dos and don'ts that were meant to ensure our safety; this was indeed a brief overview, intended to get us through until more detailed discussions could be held a few days later. He explained that anti-American feelings were running high. Attention to safety was of paramount concern. Despite my weariness, I felt a tingle of excitement. After several hours in the stifling briefing hut, we were totally spent. But there was more.

Following dismissal, we were greeted by Senior Nurse Corps Officer Comdr. Florence Alwyn. In her early forties, Commander Alwyn was a pretty brunette with a pixie hairstyle and a neat and crisp look that defied the early morning steam bath. As she greeted each of us, she seemed intelligent, highly refined, and assured, as one would expect of someone in her capacity. There is sometimes a quality—a degree of aloofness—present in chief nurses. Flo Alwyn had this quality. She understood that she was our chief nurse, and despite her friendliness there remained a cool, professional reserve.

Flo explained that Senior Medical Officer Capt. Louis Gens had invited us to lunch at his billet, located in downtown Saigon. Deferring a bath and some sleep, we piled into sedans and headed toward the city. During the five-mile drive, we had our first look at a city under martial law; we had an opportunity to see for ourselves the situation described in the official booklets.

Concertinas of barbed wire formed barricades. We saw tanks and armored personnel carriers at every major street corner. Battle-dressed ARVN troops patrolled the streets. It seemed as though something extraordinary could happen at any moment. The nightly news at home had broadcast many of these same striking images. The living-room effect was not, however, the same as being there.

French influence was everywhere. Old stucco buildings bordered sweeping boulevards. We motored past the grand French opera house, now in use as the South Vietnamese National Assembly building. Peugeots and tiny Renaults clogged the streets. French-style cafés and restaurants were stirring to life. Some signs were still in French.

Less than a decade earlier, on 8 May 1954, the French were crushingly defeated at Dien Bien Phu. This battle ended their control of the colony of French Indochina, which included the territory to be divided, in 1955, into North and South Vietnam. It was, however, difficult to erase the influence of the French because of their successful exploitation of the region for a number of years. For their part—represented by a colony of some seven thousand as I arrived in South Vietnam—the French themselves had a hard time letting go, financially and commercially.

Several elections to reunify Vietnam had been scheduled for 1956 but never took place, because South Vietnam claimed it was not bound by the conditions of the Geneva Conference that followed the fall of Dien Bien Phu. Meanwhile, Ho Chi Minh, leader of North Vietnam and a brilliant Communist strategist, threatened to replace budding Vietnamese nationalism with his own brand of Communism. The complex political maneuvering of the South Vietnamese government, backed by the French, had achieved questionable results. If Communism was to be stopped, American forces had to become involved.

There was great anticipation as I faced the prospect of playing even a minor role in this extremely significant geopolitical drama. I was there as a U.S. naval officer and as a nurse. I couldn't help feeling that this assignment would provide me with the best of both worlds—service through Navy nursing and a real chance to witness history being made.

It was our job to assist in making the transition from a small dispensary to a 100-bed, fully equiped U.S. Naval Station Hospital, under the command of Headquarters Support Activity, Saigon. During Captain Gens's luncheon we were treated to a brief history of the attempts to find a suitable building for the hospital. The government of the Republic of Vietnam wanted the U.S. presence to keep a low profile. Officials asked that the American flag fly only over the embassy and the ambassador's villa. President Ngo Dinh Diem said he was concerned that Americans would be too visible occupying new modern structures, flying their flags, making easy targets. But the more likely reason was that the government of South Vietnam did not want to appear too dependent on the United States. Since the government would not permit construction of a hospital, an "acceptable" facility had been leased. Apparently this hadn't been easy to do.

Located at 263 Tran Hung Dao near downtown Saigon, the facility would provide, for the first time, full inpatient and outpatient capability for supporting U.S. forces in South Vietnam's II Corps and IV Corps. These areas included Saigon and the Mekong Delta. We would also be responsible for treating U.S. Embassy staff; members of the Agency for International Development; and allied military personnel from Australia, New Zealand, the Philippines, and South Korea—and Vietnamese civilians, when possible.

Captain Gens and Flo provided us with numerous details that helped sate our curiosity about the hospital; we craved information and were eager to begin work there. Of course that was because we hadn't yet seen it. Sadly for all of us, our high hopes for a state-of-the-art, modern medical facility were not to be realized. Captain Gens stated flatly, "We did the best we could. Now we're stuck with it." U.S. Naval Station Hospital, Saigon, as a physical structure, left a lot to be desired. It was a credit to the staff that it emerged as the finest military medical facility in Vietnam.

Tweedie, Elaine, Jan, and Carleda were driven to their temporary quarters at the ancient, moldy, ironically named Majestic Hotel. They would have to stay at this fleabag hotel at the foot of Tu Do Street until the rotation of military personnel opened up space elsewhere. From the distance of a quarter of a century, I'm amused, but at the time a billet at the Majestic Hotel was no laughing matter. Besides the depressing state

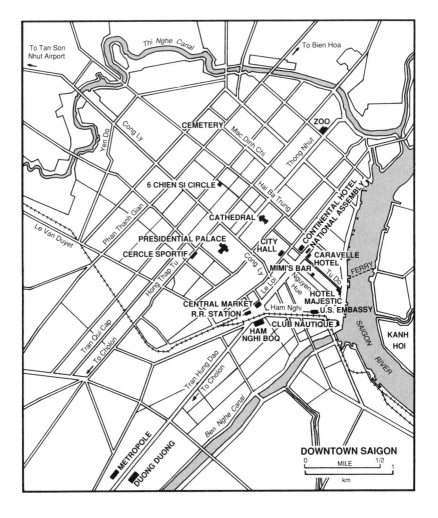

DOWNTOWN SAIGON

of the building, there were inconveniences such as hand-washing laundry in a small sink and going to the Brink (junior officer's BOQ), some distance away, for most meals; no, life was not easy at the Majestic.

I was taken to the Ham Nghi (pronounced Hom Nee) BOQ, where I would share a suite with Flo and Penny Kauffman; two days later, Tweedie joined us. Penny was in quarters when Flo and I arrived. I was struck immediately by Penny's diminutiveness. Missing the height requirement by an inch or two, she had had to sign a waiver for admission to the Navy Nurse Corps. In her mid-thirties, she had bright red hair and a generous amount of freckles. She was soft-spoken, and I would find her a little difficult to know, despite our close quarters.

Ham Nghi BOQ, overlooking the Saigon Central Market; our suite was on the top floor.

Compared with many others, our apartment was quite comfortable and, located on the seventh floor, or "deck," would conveniently offer a bird's-eye view of many stirring events in the months to come. The building was situated directly across the traffic circle from Saigon's big Central Market. Seven streets merged at the circle. The hub consisted of a small park with perfectly maintained lawns, beds of tropical flowers, and shade trees. Sidewalk benches were plentiful. Eventually the tranquillity would shatter with the onset of numerous violent events—student protests, terrorist attacks, monk burnings.

The suite consisted of three bedrooms, two bathrooms ("heads" to us), living room, dinette, small kitchen, and balcony. The furniture was typically tropical, constructed of bamboo and rattan. There were no rugs (which would only encourage the general moldiness), just bare tile decks. Large windows opened in all the rooms. These windows were without screens, a constant annoyance because of the huge mosquitoes and other flying weirdies. Our beds were no more than wooden slats, each set covered with a two-inch-thick slab of foam rubber. Each of us

Thi Ba standing on the bare tile floor of the living room at Ham Nghi

had a dressing table, which doubled as a desk, and a wardrobe. We had learned from Flo's letter to keep a light burning in the wardrobe, a trick to stem the mildew and mold that thrived in shoes.

The head presented a challenge. The room was tiny and the fixtures had seen better days. I became skilled at toilet repairs. Bent paper clips were wondrous things; they held the well-worn works together for awhile. Sooner or later my makeshift repairs would rust apart, and water-bucket hauling would be a prerequisite for using the toilet.

Our kitchen was modest. A small refrigerator and stove dominated what little space there was for food preparation. Behind the kitchen was a sort of utility room. Clothes were washed by hand in a deep sink and hung from clotheslines on the building roof. Buckets, brooms, mops, and cleaning supplies were all stowed in this tiny space.

We employed two Vietnamese women. Thi Cong, a middle-age woman, served as our laundress; Thi Ba, also middle-age, was our cook. They shared cleaning chores.

Later, during formal orientation, we learned that Westerners had to exercise prudence and caution in hiring help. It was not uncommon for Viet Cong (VC) agents to be employed by unsuspecting military personnel. Thi Cong soon troubled us. By the time we arrived, she had been in Flo's employ for five months. Slight, hollow-chested, and stoop-shouldered, she appeared in poor health. A deep productive chest cough concerned me. But our greatest worry was that she might be Viet Cong. Thi Ba was robust by comparison. Possessed of an infectious giggle, she was friendly, open, and a pleasure to be around. Her skills as a cook turned out to be just average, but she knew our likes and dislikes. I would arrive home and find Thi Ba with a cup of hot coffee ready for me. She is one of my most pleasurable memories of Saigon.

Although they were not apparent when I first arrived at my new quarters, I was soon to be introduced to geckos. We were never without these little house guests. Growing up to three inches in length and colored a pinkish blue, geckos resembled lizards. It was bad luck to kill them: they consumed vast quantities of mosquitoes and many other tropical bugs. During the day, they hid behind picture frames, inside wall cracks, and in other nooks and crannies. They appeared at night only—and then to make clicking noises. A chorus of geckos properly tuned up interrupted my sleep many nights.

Tweedie finally moved into the suite two days later and was quite happy to vacate the unaccommodating Majestic. Jan, Elaine, and Carleda stayed on there for several more weeks until quarters became available in the Brink BOQ.

The Brink ultimately suffered from the growing violence in the city. On Christmas Eve 1964, scarcely a month after our return to the States, Viet Cong saboteurs blew it up. Two were killed, and 100 military personnel, including 4 Navy nurses, were injured. The heroic young nurses made their way from the smoking ruins to the courtyard below, where they administered first aid to the injured. They accompanied the first ambulances to the hospital, where they continued treating the numerous casualties.

Capt. Rosario Fisichella later said, "The fact that they were hurt themselves, but working on others, had a tremendous morale effect on both the patients and hospital staff." The nurses refused treatment of their wounds until all the injured had been cared for. Lts. Ruth A. Mason, Frances L. Crumpton, and Barbara J. Wooster, and Lt. (jg) Ann Darby Reynolds became the first nurses to receive Purple Heart medals during the Vietnam War.

On Monday morning, 16 September 1963, we began our check-in procedures and briefings and reported to the commanding officer at Head-

The author, Tweedie Searcy, Elaine King, Jan Barcott, and Carleda Lorberg head toward their initial briefing after arrival in Vietnam.

quarters Support Activity (HedSuppAct), Saigon. This command was housed in a former cigarette factory located in Cholon, about five miles from Saigon. The process was similar to any other Navy check-in procedure, including the logging in of orders, turning in of pay records to the disbursing office, and finalizing of billeting arrangements.

Following this process, we headed back toward Saigon. Stopping at the dispensary, we were introduced to staff members and had our first look at the facility and the patients. After lunch, our first day's briefings began in earnest.

At that time, all military personnel entering Vietnam for duty received a three-day orientation. Since we had been given a Secret security clearance (the second-highest level), the material that we were presented was sensitive. Because our group was large (eighty-five military personnel), the lectures were held downtown, in the Capitol Kinh Do Theatre, rather than at Military Assistance Advisory Group Headquarters (known as MAAG). Several days earlier, the MAAG compound had been a Viet Cong target. A thirty-foot section of the surrounding wall was blown out. The Kinh Do, leased and controlled by the American armed forces, was considered relatively safe.

Rooms with a View

The command center of Headquarters Support Activity, Saigon, in Cholon

It was the responsibility of the Army to conduct the briefings. Maj. Gen. Charles J. Timmes, MAAG commander, was the featured speaker. He was of special interest to the Navy nurses because his brother, Capt. J.J. Timmes, Medical Corps, USN (Ret.), was a well-known Navy thoracic surgeon.

General Timmes addressed every group arriving in Vietnam, and his words were highly inspirational. As he progressed, we found him to be an accomplished and dynamic speaker. As he turned our attention to some of the political and military aspects of U.S. involvement, General Timmes held us all in rapt attention. He left little doubt in our minds that if Ho Chi Minh's efforts to unify North and South Vietnam under a single flag succeeded, that flag would be a Communist one. In order to accomplish this goal, Ho Chi Minh's next move would be to provoke civil war, General Timmes believed. I recalled one basic Marxist-Leninist line: a relatively few, hard-core people, ambitious and without scruples, can force their will upon many. General Timmes impressed upon us that this incursion into South Vietnam had to be stopped. That was exactly why all eighty-five of us were there. His speech provoked many sobering thoughts.

Two more days of intense briefings followed. Several speakers addressed our group on topics that expanded mainly upon how to deport ourselves in Vietnam. Constant attention to cultural standards couldn't be overemphasized. No one was to act offensively, by use of disrespectful language or blatant disregard for local customs, in the presence of Vietnamese nationals. During my experience, I noted only a few digressions from this policy.

Personal safety was now discussed in depth. Unlike conventional troops waging war on the battlefield, the Viet Cong terrorist, we learned, waged his battle in unremarkable dress—perhaps traditional black pajamas, or the ragtag garb of a *cyclopousse* driver, or the shirt and tie of a Vietnamese national employed by a foreign government. It seemed that he wore many faces, appearing almost anywhere. The city, I heard, was his battleground.

We were advised to avoid crowds. If we found ourselves in a crowd, we were to stay alert, to "watch our six"—meaning be aware of what was happening behind us—an expression borrowed from combat aviators, who spoke of the opposite of twelve o'clock as a dangerous blind spot. We were warned to stay in small groups of two or three when off duty, and to do nothing to attract attention to ourselves.

Leaving orientation behind, our duties began at the American Dispensary. Our time was consumed with caring for patients, checking and ordering supplies, familiarizing ourselves with equipment, getting to know the staff and civilian employees, and countless other tasks. The transition from dispensary to hospital was under way.

THREE

Moving toward Commissioning

ON 27 SEPTEMBER, all American Dispensary inpatients were either evacuated to the Army's Eighth Field Hospital at Nha Trang, the Philippines, or discharged to their billets. We were given ninety-six hours—until 1 October—to pack up all of the dispensary gear, move it, and be ready to receive patients at our new facility two or three miles across town. I was living in dungarees and sneakers nearly twenty-four hours a day. We packed and inventoried everything from dressings to Darvon and moved the portable X-ray machine, surgical equipment, tables, beds, linens, urinals, and bedpans. The task often seemed overwhelming.

The new hospital—that is, the main inpatient facility—was formerly an old apartment house. By the time the Navy had narrowed down the list of sites to three, this dirty, broken-down edifice seemed to stand head and shoulders above the rest. What could the losers have been like, we wondered. Among other things, it was not large enough to house the labs and outpatient clinic, which had to be located across the street.

The Vietnamese government had at least permitted the Navy to construct a new, air-conditioned building of cement and corrugated metal to house the Emergency and Operating rooms adjacent to the converted apartment building. Since this 1500-square-foot structure was new, it was clean—which was more than could be said of the main building.

The filth and squalor there were beyond belief. The local construction help relieved themselves at will all over the decks of the heads, which were not in working order. Though these areas were cleaned daily, by the next day's inspection they were once again littered with human waste.

What could the workers do? We soon found that the antiquated state of the plumbing didn't matter, because there was no water. It was the dry season. The occasional rain shower filled big tin cans, providing our only source. There were neither cleaning agents nor a profusion of rags. After two days we were ready to turn in our mops and board the first aircraft out.

Instead, we became masters at improvisation. As a Navy Seabees' expression put it, "We have done so much with so little for so long that now we can do anything with nothing forever."

At the outset, another huge problem was the language barrier. Among us nurses, only Flo spoke serviceable French; none of us spoke Vietnamese. The Vietnamese language was an extremely difficult one to learn for two reasons: it was monosyllabic and tonal. A word, depending on how it was said, could have several meanings. (Symbols found over the letters indicated the tone differences.)

It was a challenge. Still, we strove to communicate. Both at work and at our quarters, Vietnamese civilians were speaking to us and we found ourselves beginning to use their words and phrases. None of us, however, ever mastered conversational Vietnamese.

If this barrier was equally frustrating to the Vietnamese, they never expressed it the way we did. Our frustration sometimes got the better of us. But the gentle Vietnamese remained taciturn. In the end I found a way to communicate by using French, Vietnamese, pidgin English, and sign language—all in one sentence.

The main facility at our new site had five stories. The elevator, another antique, did not work. This meant that everything from syringes to hospital beds had to be hauled up flights of narrow stairs. Unwieldy objects had to be turned on their sides or ends. Later, even stretchers bearing patients were turned on their ends to accommodate the stairs. The effort was exhausting.

The switchboard from the dispensary was relocated to the new facility. Miss Ninh, our telephone operator, spoke tolerable English. An attractive young woman, she possessed many skills in art and music and had earned a law degree. She had chosen employment as our switchboard operator because it provided a better salary than what she could receive practicing law in Vietnam. Miss Ninh helped us often when the language barrier seemed insurmountable, but the switchboard itself was another monumental frustration. This old dinosaur of communications technology was of World War I vintage and forever blowing its fuses in the effort to relay calls through a maze of switchboards and

The converted apartment building that became the new inpatient facility, and the Metropole, across the boulevard—part quarters, part outpatient building for U.S. Naval Station Hospital, Saigon

operators named Tiger, Deadly, Weasel, Moonshine, and Sky King. The entire system malfunctioned constantly, presenting a communications barrier of a purely mechanical kind.

Still, we persevered. We cleared the trash from, swept, and swabbed five stories of decks. Space for 100 beds had been cleaned and sanitized to the best of our ability. The hospital furnishings, bedside lockers, chairs, tables, cabinets, and other equipment had been wiped down, hauled in, and put in place. Tweedie and her corpsmen had, in relative air-conditioned luxury, put together spartan but acceptable Emergency and Operating rooms. Since they didn't have to deal with stairs, Tweedie's group was probably the least exhausted among us.

Working so hard in the oppressive heat and humidity, with little to drink, left us somewhat dehydrated and seriously drained of energy. But by 1000 hours on 1 October 1963, a formerly dilapidated apartment building had been transformed into a respectable medical-treatment facility. It was commissioning day.

Our official title was the U.S. Naval Station Hospital, Saigon, Republic of Vietnam, under the command of Headquarters Support Activity, Saigon. The early morning ceremony was held in the sun-washed courtyard, where a podium and a microphone had been set up. Bright bouquets of tropical flowers added splashes of color. A blue-and-gold ribbon stretched across the entrance, waiting to be cut. Perhaps twenty people from the various agencies attended.

The entire hospital staff, for the first time dressed in white uniforms, mustered in ranks for the ceremony. There were 103 personnel in attendance, making an impressive-looking group of doctors, nurses, and hospital corpsmen. We sparkled in our ward-white uniforms (for nurses) and tropical-dress whites with service ribbons (for men). After the ceremony, we took a few moments to admire each other in such splendid attire. After all, for the past ninety-six hours we had seen nothing but sweat-soaked fatigues and grimy dungarees.

The staff consisted of eighteen officers, including Medical Corps, Nurse Corps, and Medical Service Corps; seventy-nine enlisted hospital corpsmen; five civilian Thai registered nurses; and one registered nurse employed by the State Department and attached to the embassy. Breaking stride with government policy, we were unable to employ Vietnamese nationals to supplement the Navy nurse staff—unfortunately, those nurses' local training was at the time substandard. Consequently, since patient care transcended all other considerations, Thai nurses were recruited from Bangkok. They had been trained at the American Missionary Hospital there and spoke and wrote English reasonably well. They were, as a group, very conscientious and reliable and proved to be a joy to work with, a total delight in every way.

The embassy nurse's duties were similar to those of a public-health nurse. In the mornings she and the embassy doctor would assist in our outpatient clinic. Many of the patients were staff from the embassy or from other civilian agencies and expressed relatively minor complaints. We were available to help the embassy medical personnel if needed, and they in turn provided support for us during emergencies by offering extra sets of hands.

We felt adequately covered in all medical areas. Unfortunately, this condition was to be short-lived. Within a few months, Secretary of Defense Robert McNamara spearheaded recommendations that left us with a 20 percent reduction in our corpsmen staff. Classified as noncombatants, hospital corpsmen were grouped with clerical assistants and the like. When the recommendation for across-the-board reduction of noncombatant personnel was made, our hospital was hit hard. We all took a dim view of this; in our opinion hospital corpsmen were not the

Pat Panasthain ("Miss Pat"), one of the Thai nurses who supplemented staff at the new hospital

same as secretaries and clerks. Happily, this situation was eventually resolved with reinstatement of the corpsmen.

During the commissioning ceremony, appropriate remarks were offered by several people, including Capt. Malcolm Friedman, commanding officer of HedSuppAct, and Capt. Louis Gens, our senior medical officer. Afterward the ribbon was cut by Maj. Gen. Richard C. Weede, USMC, chief of staff at Military Assistance Command, Vietnam. Finger foods and beverages followed the ribbon-cutting, and for about an hour we socialized. It was the *last* social occasion at that hospital. Somewhere a firefight was in progress, and we were open for business.

Following commissioning, we experienced nine days of normal hospital routine. My assigned duty was to supervise the ICU and the Recovery Room. Subject to change due to circumstances, my A.M. shift lasted from 0700 until 1530; if an emergency occurred, shifts were extended for as long as necessary. My staff consisted of a senior corpsman and three additional corpsmen.

Our first patient, a field soldier, received the unexciting diagnosis of hemorrhoids. To be sure, the soldier didn't find his condition uninteresting, but we had all been hoping for something a little more dramatic. Our second patient, an officer with the provost marshal's staff in Saigon, suffered from severe multiple carbuncles on the back of the neck.

On 10 October, we received our first wounded in action (WIA). The A.M. staff was ready to secure for the day; the afternoon shift was aboard to take over the watch. A message from Tan Son Nhut's Flight Operations informed us of an inbound helicopter medical air evacuation flight with a severely wounded man aboard. Tweedie, as nurse anesthetist, and I remained on duty to await his arrival.

Within a half hour the ambulance arrived bearing the injured soldier. A blood-soaked battle dressing covered a bullet wound in the hip area. I noted immediately that this man was a sergeant and a member of the elite U.S. Army Special Forces, a wearer of the famous green beret. Though in severe pain, he remained stoic throughout his surgical procedure.

The effect of an injection of morphine in the field lingered and controlled his pain somewhat. As I cut away his dirty, bloody uniform and prepped him for surgery, we were able to talk. He had been on jungle patrol for twenty-four hours. While returning, just one mile from camp, his squad was ambushed. The sergeant and several ARVN troops were wounded by small-arms fire. A single bullet entering high on the posterior hip area penetrated the pelvic girdle, inflicting a through-and-through wound of the colon. The progress of the bullet was halted by the wing of the pelvis on the opposite side.

Necessitated by the nature of the wound, a low-abdominal exploratory incision with repair of several damaged intraabdominal sites was followed by a higher temporary colostomy. On completion of these two operative procedures, he was turned on his side to clean and debride the penetration site. His lying on his back exerted enough pressure on the wound to prevent serious bleeding. When this pressure was removed (by turning him on his side), the initial probing of the wound resulted in severe hemorrhage and shock.

Tweedie pumped blood into him at a greater rate than he lost it. As a result, we succeeded in reducing his state of shock. As his blood pressure began to rise and as his pulse volume, rate, and rhythm improved, we all heaved a sigh of relief. The surgeon was able to determine that an artery had been nicked by the bullet. The hemorrhage was controlled, the wound packed, and we were able to close the case.

An Army sergeant's life was saved because of a Navy surgical team's expertise—and because an adequate facility existed in Saigon. The lim-

Tweedie and surgeon Lt. Comdr. Walter Johnson

ited hospital facilities prior to our arrival had forced all major hospital cases to be flown to Clark Air Force Base Hospital in the Philippines. The soldier would not have survived if it had been necessary to med-evac him to the Philippines. I was especially pleased with the perfor-mance of the team—it marked the first time we had worked together.

Our team surgeon, Lt. Comdr. Walter Johnson, was highly skilled and well trained. His calm demeanor served us well that day, during our first combat-casualty admission. I worked often with Walt during my Saigon tour and never viewed him as anything less than a consummate professional.

The sergeant remained in the ICU for twenty-eight days. He was a model patient, and many of the staff became attached to him. Finally he was medevaced to Clark for closure of his temporary colostomy, as there was a Command policy that any patient requiring over thirty days' medical care be transferred. As a combat-casualty facility, we were not equipped to handle cases of long duration.

This young Special Forces soldier made a solid recovery. As I saw him off in the ambulance to Tan Son Nhut, he placed in my hand an object, something I treasure to this day. It was his green beret. Months after he left our hospital, his mother sent us a box of fudge and a letter expressing her appreciation for the care he had received. This gesture touched us deeply and we felt richly rewarded. A year later, as I was being detached from my tour of duty, the sergeant dropped by to see us. He was beginning his *third* tour of duty, a not-uncommon event in the early days of the Vietnam conflict.

From the day he first arrived at our door, the casualties never ceased— and they began to increase proportionately to the escalation of the war effort. My sense of our work, day to day, was that our success in saving lives was phenomenal. The major reasons for this success were the rapid transport by helicopter of the injured and the fact that we at the new U.S. Naval Station Hospital, Saigon, were there to receive them.

FOUR

Duong Duong

THERE WAS A SAYING in Vietnam: *dien cai dau*. We Americans just said "dinky dow." Translated, *dien cai dau* meant "crazy." Naval Station Hospital, Saigon, was one dinky dow place. One of the early indications of just how crazy things were going to get was the controversy over our hospital shingle. It hung above the doorway and read Duong Duong. Our pronunciation of it led to the nickname Dong Dong. The mystery sign was an aggravation for a short while. No one could figure out what it meant. We consulted a dictionary without success. Even our Vietnamese staff shook their heads in bewilderment when asked to translate. Eventually our curiosity subsided, and we did end up with a proper sign, U.S. Naval Station Hospital, Saigon, hung nearby. The nickname stuck, however; the shingle remained. I continued to worry that our sign might have been a prank or that it had been intended for some other shop or warehouse somewhere in the city. It remained an unsolved mystery and a symbol of the dinky dow place our hospital was to become.

Duong Duong turned out to be a particularly awkward facility. Of all the medical facilities I have been privileged to work in, I have never experienced anything like that one. Virtually nothing at our new hospital was easily accessible. Even the Army's Eighth Field Hospital in Nha Trang, essentially a tent facility, was more workable than Duong Duong. We paid for the intervention of South Vietnamese politics and discomfort over the U.S. presence in Saigon, which forced us to lease rather than build a facility.

Directly behind Duong Duong's main five-story inpatient building stood the new Emergency and Operating facility. Close by, four small corrugated metal sheds had been erected to house supplies and equip-

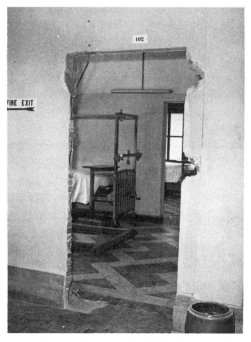

Finishing touches still to be done on the ICU. Note the deck, a reminder of the apartment-house origins of the hospital.

ment. A parking lot for ambulances, cars, and the hospital utility vehicle stood just inside the gate. A cement security wall with a main gate and three observation towers completed the compound.

The inpatient hospital was set up in the following fashion: Intensive Care and Recovery units with a sixteen-bed capacity, first deck; Surgical Ward, second deck; Medical Ward, third deck; Convalescent Ward, fourth deck; and a conference room and later a small PX, fifth deck.

The majority of my duties occurred on the first deck, where the situation in the ICU was unique. Most of my experience in ICUs had been in smaller hospitals that had wards where all patients could be observed simultaneously. The Saigon hospital ICU had a larger capacity, but the patients were housed in eight separate rooms. Instant viewing was impossible. Consequently, there was a great deal of legwork for my corpsmen and me. And we soon found that such legwork would leave us exhausted if the patient load was heavy. Fortunately, this inconvenience never resulted in the loss of a patient in the ICU. Staffing was such that I was able to adequately provide for observation and nursing care of my

Duong Duong

Corpsman Bill McKenna's baby Malaysian sunbear opened the zoo at Duong Duong.

patients at all times. Nevertheless, providing care in a maze was difficult.

There was an unusual feature on the fourth deck. In addition to housing the convalescing patients, it also provided a special kind of patient therapy. So many of our normal hospital activities were, by virtue of our special conditions, somewhat unorthodox, or, as we liked to say, "dinky dow." It therefore didn't seem abnormal to provide our patients with a small "zoo" for diversion.

Our zoo was not planned, but sort of evolved after one of our hospital corpsmen adopted a baby Malaysian sunbear that he couldn't keep in his quarters. Ordinarily this situation might be frowned upon by most hospital administrations. However, the appealing tiny baby needed frequent feedings, and there was a distinct scarcity of activities to help convalescing patients pass the time. So I found a way to stretch the rules.

Animal tending turned out to be a popular form of therapy. The patients enjoyed the responsibility of bottle-feeding the cub regularly every four hours and even set their clocks so that they could arise at night for a feeding. Sadly, after several days the sunbear died. He was soon replaced by a civet kitten a soldier we were treating had found in the jungle. The animal, wandering alone, had seemed helpless, and the soldier had picked it up, tucking it inside his fatigue pants pocket. After recovering, the soldier returned to the field—with his civet. Another young soldier, in for a series of diagnostic tests, brought in a tiny monkey who had jumped on his shoulder while he was on jungle patrol. The monkey protested loudly when someone attempted to separate him from his surrogate parent. Still, we provided it foster care. This unorthodox facility remained a favorite feature—until the patient with the baby python was admitted. Then the administration decided to close the zoo. Therapy or not, the order was: No more pets!

General hospital supplies, such as crutches, bed frames, and all of our cast supplies, were housed in the Central Supply shed. Another shed held our steam autoclaves and water sterilizer. Sterile supplies, such as surgical packs, trauma trays, and abdominal trays, occupied the third building. The fourth shed contained the emergency generator that supplied electricity to the Emergency and Operating rooms. The rest of us, in the event of a power outage, made do with battery-powered battle lanterns.

Our "cast room" was one of a kind. It was the open-air space near the sheds. Crates and later a green park bench were used to simulate a hospital cast table. The injured patient would take a seat and the cast would be applied. Even during the monsoon season, patients, holding big umbrellas, were treated in this open-air space by technicians who did their best to keep plaster and cast materials dry.

Central Supply had many functions. The CSR technician worked in the open air as well. All soiled instruments, trays, tubing, flasks, syringes, and other equipment were wheeled to this area on an old gurney. Using big basins set atop the gurney, the tech would wash and scrub the equipment. At the end of the gurney stood the standard operating-room double-basin holder, which held the rinse basins.

The open-air facilities were novel enough during the dry season, but the onset of the monsoon season presented real problems for the CSR tech as well. He could be seen standing before his basins, elbow-deep in soiled, bloodied equipment, scouring away in the midst of a downpour. While scrubbing instruments in the pouring rain was an annoyance in some ways, it did have a singular benefit. Since there was no lack of fresh water, the tech didn't have to trek to the spigots to constantly refill the basins. It seemed to us that during the rainy season at Duong Duong, the uniform of the day for the CSR techs should have been bathing suit and shower shoes. Even the corrugated metal roof that eventually was erected over the area did little to keep a blowing rain from soaking everything.

Duong Duong became many things to us. It became a source of great satisfaction and pride but also a continuous source of frustration. The

At the outdoor Central Supply, Joe Craney ("Mr. Clean") doing his best during a monsoon

language barrier was problematic, the physical layout was, at best, awkward, and the switchboard was a vexation. But nothing beat our elevator.

In a five-story medical facility, an elevator isn't merely a convenience, it's a necessity. For the first three months that our hospital was

One of the four guard towers and the staff motor pool inside the hospital compound; once, a sniper fired from the building on the right.

operating, we didn't have a working elevator. Early on, it was determined that the elevator motor could not handle the weight of a patient, gurney, and attendant. After three months, the problem was solved—almost—with the arrival of a new motor, but it kept burning out and replacement parts were difficult to come by. For weeks on end, the sounds of clanking, banging, and groaning of cables shattered the tranquillity of our hospital environment. This was a particularly serious problem in the Recovery Room, which was adjacent to the elevator shaft on first deck. Often, as I was attending a patient in Recovery—taking a blood pressure or determining if the patient was oriented—all hell would suddenly break loose in the elevator shaft.

Even when the elevator worked, it was unreliable. It would stop at the correct deck only to jerk suddenly upward or downward, leaving the occupants stranded between decks. On one occasion when I was stuck on the elevator I climbed atop a gurney, to be lifted through the hatch in the roof by two corpsmen who had been alerted by my cries for help. As I emerged, soiled and rumpled, I decided that elevator escape was quite literally above and beyond the "normal" call of duty.

It *was* within the normal call of duty to improvise. Fracture beds are a necessity in any hospital. We had frames for four fracture beds. Unfortunately we had no weights or line. Friends at the military air base at Tan Son Nhut stepped in to help. Liberated, or *cumshawed,* from the parachute loft, nylon rope was sent over to us. We then had first-class nylon traction line. Weights were another thing. Since we had none, I devised a system of water-filled buckets as weights. After discovering that the

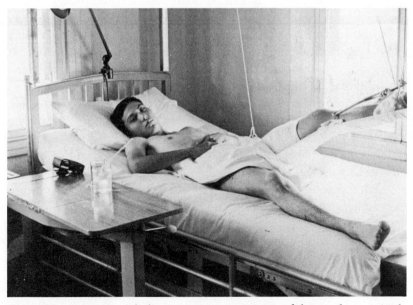

Patient Ken Fujimoto, a helicopter gunner, was one of those who required our brick-bucket weights.

water used in the buckets was evaporating, I looked for another solution. We had a brick pile on the compound: bricks became weights, and our Vietnamese help had no trouble realizing that being handed an empty bucket meant it was time to go to the brick pile. No need for sign language or awkward translations.

The demand for constant improvisation was indeed frustrating, but it was also rewarding to see just how resourceful we could be. Empty intravenous bottles and tubing became drinking containers and straws. The IV bottles also became urinary drainage bottles. Discarded tin cans found further use as small-item storage containers. Howitzer shell casings of 105 mm made excellent, heavy flower vases. Even unwieldy gladioli could be safely contained in these shell casings. This eliminated the frequent messes that occurred when someone accidentally knocked over a flower arrangement.

While none of these vexations were necessarily life-threatening, the problems with our oxygen and anesthesia gases certainly were. We had on hand two dozen G cylinders, the tall green canisters carrying under pressure about 2,200 pounds of pure oxygen each. A number of smaller cylinders hooked onto the anesthesia machines. As a cylinder was emptied, it was placed in the group of tanks to be trucked into Saigon for refill at a local gas company. The service rendered by this company deteriorated from poor to intolerable. Tanks were being returned marked full when in fact they had not been refilled. Tanks sent one day should have been returned the following day. However, this was not done. In one emergency situation, Tweedie experienced a sick feeling when she realized that the nitrous oxide tank she was using was empty.

It became evident that our supplier could not be trusted. As a result, Tweedie arranged with Air Force friends at Tan Son Nhut to have the cylinders flown to Clark Air Force Base for refill. The tanks made the 2,000-mile round-trip to Clark faster than they made the 6-mile round-trip to Saigon—and they returned full every time.

Another source of frustration was our supply system. It was inconsistent at best. We found that orders of a rush priority took weeks to arrive, while orders of a lower priority arrived surprisingly fast. As soon as our hospital opened, the ordering of supplies was under way, based on a three-month usage rate. Since this was a brand-new effort, there were no past records upon which to base projections. Consequently, Tweedie had to wing it.

An example of problems in the system occurred early on. Sixteen cases of ABDs had been ordered. An ABD is a frequently used type of surgical dressing made up of an eight-by-ten-inch square of absorbent material encased in a layer of gauze. After a prolonged period, we received a cable from the Navy Supply Center in the States asking us if we knew how many aircraft would be needed to ship sixteen tons of the featherweight ABDs. Somewhere along the way in processing the nine copies of the request, Tweedie's order had been changed from cases to tons. That clerical error caused a few laughs and a whole lot of annoyance.

The main hospital compound—the inpatient facility—was located on the south side of a highly congested six-lane boulevard, Tran Hung Dao. Tran Hung Dao was the major artery connecting Saigon with its sister city, Cholon. It also effectively bisected Duong Duong. On the north side of Tran Hung Dao, the remainder of the hospital—outpatient and diagnostic facilities—was located on the first two decks of the Metropole Bachelor Enlisted Quarters. Door to door, the hospital was separated by two hundred feet of speeding traffic, and we had to steer patients up and down the sidewalk and across the boulevard to the other side. We did this often: across the street were our laboratory for blood chemistries, urinalyses, and other tests; the X-ray Department; pharmacy; Immunization Room; outpatient clinic; and personnel offices.

A typical case would involve a patient needing X-rays. On the south side of the street, the bedridden patient was strapped to a litter, then turned on end to make it down the stairs. Transferred to a gurney, the patient was then wheeled out of the compound, onto the sidewalk, then up the sidewalk, across three lanes of traffic through an opening in the island, then across another three lanes of traffic to the north side. Then the patient had to be wheeled further down the sidewalk and finally into the Metropole. The whole process took at least twenty minutes—depending, of course, on traffic.

The monsoon season complicated things even more. Many times I observed a speeding gurney carrying a patient swathed head to toe in billowing plastic sheeting. Sometimes, if the patient was strong enough, he was covered in plastic to his neck and somehow managed to hold a big, black umbrella over his own head as well as the corpsman's.

After the first month, we were assigned our own Vietnamese traffic policeman. He took his life into his hands every time he darted into the street to stop traffic. I'm sure he often noted the dazed, frightened look of a patient caught in the middle of the speeding Saigon traffic. No doubt the patient had to suppress his panic and resist the urge to leap from the gurney and run for his life. It was a dinky dow system, but we did what we had to do.

While coping with our share of innovative solutions to Duong Duong's idiosyncracies, a daily system began to emerge. This routine was, in fact, much the same as in all other Navy hospitals. We settled into a workable system not long after commissioning. Arriving by 0730, we were ready to receive Old Charley. Old Charley pushed the chow cart from a galley located one and a half blocks away. He was a small, wiry man, seemingly ancient. The steam wagon he pushed was heavy, stocked with hot food items, breads, condiments, canned fruits, and desserts—as well as all the necessary tin trays, utensils, and coffee mugs. The traditional Vietnamese garb he wore was covered by a white apron. He cheerfully stood ready to fill trays and help distribute meals if we were busy elsewhere.

While the patients had breakfast, the charge nurses received the reports from the night-duty personnel. We then prepared our corpsmen assignments. Those patients scheduled for surgery received pre-op injections before being wheeled outside to the surgery area. We routinely performed herniaplasties, hemorrhoidectomies, appendectomies, skin grafts, vein ligations, and many other kinds of minor surgical procedures.

Bed patients were bathed, linen changed, dressings changed, medications supplied, treatments carried out, rooms tidied, wards swept and swabbed, and trash emptied. In the midst of these activities, the doctors arrived to make their sick calls and write orders. This process was followed by paperwork involving the transcribing of orders on cards that were kept in a Kardex. Other cards were rewritten in the event of medication and treatment changes.

During the morning hours, the first admissions began to arrive. Depending on the number of admissions, this could create a lot of ward-assigning, orders, routine admission procedures, and, of course, additional paperwork. Patients then began to return from the OR. Since I was in charge of ICU and Recovery, my corpsmen and I were suddenly very busy monitoring these patients.

It became essential to square away my unit early. Scarcely a day passed without a visiting VIP. Gen. William C. Westmoreland was the commander of the Military Assistance Command, Vietnam (MACV) during my Saigon duty. The general was a soldier's soldier. He was tall, slender, gray at the temples, with penetrating black eyes peering from beneath thick black eyebrows. Though warm and friendly, he also had a

Duong Duong

Kitsy Westmoreland and Izzy Klingenhagen, two of the reliable, invaluable Gray Ladies

sober side. We liked and respected the general immensely. Despite their hectic schedules, Ambassador Henry Cabot Lodge and General Westmoreland were regulars, visiting critically injured, ill, and recuperating soldiers. Often, Purple Hearts were presented at bedside. TV cameramen along with photojournalists and reporters appeared regularly to film and report on our activities.

Between 1100 and 1200, Old Charley arrived with noon chow. Then, during midafternoon, one of the highlights of our daily routine occurred. They were called the Gray Ladies. Kitsy Westmoreland, wife of the general, arrived with one or two other officers' wives. Setting up carts of fresh-baked cookies and coffee, they made their rounds of the wards. Our patients eagerly awaited the Gray Ladies, who would stop and visit, write letters for those who couldn't, and fill soldiers' shopping lists at the PX, delivering them the following day. In the thirteen months I served in Vietnam, I can only recall a couple of occasions when the Gray Ladies failed to appear. They were always gracious and generous with their time and enhanced the quality of care at Duong Duong.

The evening shift relieved us at 1530. By that time, afternoon admissions were completed. Scheduled surgeries, for the most part, had ended. Old Charley had made his last trip. The wards became quiet. Sometimes the tranquillity would end abruptly.

In emergency situations, none of us dwelled on inconveniences and vexations. No matter how long and tiring the day had been, when a crisis occurred, we were ready. After a time, we all adapted to the unexpected violence of terrorist activities. In short order, the unexpected became routine. As we became more experienced with crises, we could switch gears, mentally and physically, more quickly. We learned quickly to adapt—to live on the edge.

During the Korean War, my experience with combat casualties had been limited to nursing aboard a medevac aircraft as a Navy flight nurse. I had not worked in a situation where the wounded arrived directly from the battlefield. Instead of a stabilized patient, well enough to withstand the flight from the Far East back to the States, I was seeing men in shock, cardiac arrest, and respiratory failure. These were life-and-death situations, demanding quick and correct responses.

Routine was overtaken in a heartbeat by chaos. Carefully swabbed decks became slick with dirt and blood, piled high with bloody flak jackets, dirty, wet clothing, boots, webbing, discarded side arms, and Kabar knives—with the personal debris of war. All of us experienced an adrenaline rush that erased fatigue and sharpened senses. Inevitably, hours later, with the last wound packed and dressed, the anesthesia gases turned off, the Emergency Room doors finally closed, we all experienced a letdown.

But there was so much more to do. With soiled instruments, bloody linens, intravenous poles, suction machines, stethoscopes, blood-pressure cuffs, gas machines, and piles of discarded clothing laying about, and with sterile supplies nearly depleted, hours of work lay ahead. I often wondered if tossing a lighted match into the mess might not be the quickest solution.

As a charge nurse I knew how to organize. In twenty years of nursing experience, I had dealt with just about every aspect of trauma. Duong Duong, however, was unique. It challenged and broadened my skills. While my Korean experiences distanced me from the battlefield, Saigon would draw me nearer. Naval Station Hospital, Saigon, with all of its quirks and annoyances, was emerging as the peak of my career.

Within Duong Duong's walls we ran the gamut of emotions—from the blackest despair of watching a young soldier's life slip away, to the brightest moments when everything seemed to work and we were able to heal and save. Disconcerting and difficult days eventually were balanced by satisfying ones and by leisure.

I worked in Saigon and also lived there. The city became my home for thirteen months. Many hours off duty were spent in an environment that posed danger but held fascination. I was eager to explore and enjoy the city and to catalog my impressions.

FIVE
Exploring Saigon

READING GRAHAM GREENE's 1956 novel *The Quiet American* had provided me with countless images of Saigon and my own list of must-see places. With his remarkable gift of description, Greene painted a vivid portrait of this city of intrigue—of the Continental Hotel, of the famous Milk Bar across the square, which was one of the first VC targets, of the Foreign Legion. Saigon was lush and tropical, noisy and dirty, shimmering with waves of heat or drenched in monsoon rains. Even with its problems and dangers, the lure of this metropolis could not be resisted for long. Saigon beckoned to each of us.

Tweedie and I ventured out often, with Saigon veterans Flo Alwyn and Penny Kauffman as our guides. We were immediately struck by three things: the city's traffic, its noise, and the smell. These aspects of the Saigon environment nearly overwhelmed all else at first. Once we became accustomed to the intense dose of environmental onslaughts, the subtleties of Saigon began to emerge. But first we had to cross the street and get to the other side in one piece.

Saigon traffic was unlike any I had seen anywhere in the world. Only Tokyo came close. Vehicles of all kinds moved in every direction. In Saigon, the driver with the loudest horn came out the best at intersections.

In picturing all this, bear in mind that the population of Saigon was more than two million people. Only 203 miles of roads had been built to accommodate more than 642,000 motor vehicles registered in South Vietnam. This meant that there were more than 3,000 vehicles per mile. It was staggering.

Add to this half a million pedaled vehicles. Then add thousands of pony and ox carts, cargo and passenger *cyclopousses* (three-wheeled trishas, either pedaled or motorized), pushcarts, and hundreds of lumbering military vehicles—including tanks, armored personnel carriers, jeeps, weapons- and troop-carriers, heavy-duty trucks, station wagons, buses, and sedans. We found that survival meant learning to be nimble-footed and quick-eyed while jumping for our lives, dashing madly across intersections, and dodging vehicles.

An acquaintance employed by one of the civilian agencies in the city told me that several U.S. traffic engineers had been invited to Saigon to help solve the traffic nightmare. The story was that when the engineers inquired about the fatality rate for the city, they were given an incredibly low figure, and so they gave up and went home.

During my experience, I never saw a fatal accident. Traffic was simply too congested to allow for the sorts of high-speed situations that lead to serious injury. On the other hand, the numbers of bent fenders and smashed bicycles and motor scooters probably exceeded those of any city in the world.

Taxis were a favorite mode of transportation. The tiny blue-and-white Renaults looked like contestants in a demolition derby. Esthetics were of no importance. Fenders were bent, doors and hoods often held in place with wire or rope, and floorboards were frequently missing. Upon entering one of these cars, the prudent passenger usually first assessed the condition of the floor to avoid winding up with a foot in the street.

For entertainment, the passenger moving through the less-congested outskirts could gaze down between his feet and watch the roadway whizzing by. During the monsoon season, torrential rains swept through the streets, and the tiny taxis shipped so much water they almost required the services of a bilge pump. Imagine what happened to a military spit-and-polish shoe shine.

Once I had developed some confidence, I purchased a bicycle and frequently rode through and in and around this mass of confusion. While I was on my bike, luck was with me.

Toward the end of my tour of duty, my luck as a taxi passenger ran out. One afternoon I was traveling to work in a cab when we were struck broadside by a truck loaded with pipe. A length of pipe punched through the window, struck me in the side, and forced me up into the overhead light. A few stitches closed the head wound. I still have the scar from the rib injury, a souvenir of the hazards of motoring around Saigon.

Saigon was a city of remarkable sounds. They were common, ev-

The traffic pattern at the circle in front of Central Market

eryday sounds in this place, but they were ones that we Westerners had never heard. Doan Bich and Le Trang, authors of *Saigon in the Flesh,* describe them as the "semantics of the Saigon peddlers." They also say, "One is hard put to explain where in salesdom is the relation between the sound and the ware."

Therein lies the point. Saigon nearly vibrates with the "semimusical semantics" communicated by the city's peddlers to proclaim their arrival in the neighborhoods. Although each peddler's "song" says something, one would have to live in the city for years to be able to decipher them all. From noodles to *non las* (traditional woven straw hats), there were as many tunes as there were peddlers to "sing" them.

One of the most familiar songs was that announcing the arrival of the Chinese noodle-soup vendor. I marveled at the citizens' ability to perceive, in the din, the clacking of bamboo sticks being struck together. A small boy clothed in black cotton shorts preceded the peddler. The sound of the sticks was rhythmic—a lively, pleasing cha-cha beat.

Another curious tune was the metallic clicking of the scissors manipulated by the seller of a crisp, sweet-smelling pastry resembling funnel cake. The clicking of the oversize scissors attracted a steady stream of customers who responded to the distinctive clatter.

Pedaling down a street, an itinerant blacksmith alerted the city folk to his trade by rattling a metal chain that hung from his wrist. He could sharpen a dull knife, duplicate a key, and fix just about anything.

Bottle caps strung on a wire were shaken vigorously to call those in need of a masseur. A steamed-rice peddler arrived beating a small bongo drum. Balls suspended across the head of the drum produced a hollow-sounding tattoo when shaken. I have never heard this sound duplicated.

A curious chorus of voices—high-pitched, strident, and overwhelming to the ear—was ever present, and the chanted, spoken, shaken, rattled, and drummed sounds of Saigon identified a distinctive community of vendors. The "semimusical semantics" of these peddlers provided me with an impression that to this day is recorded in my remembrances of this exotic city.

Saigon was also a city of smells. The aromas were as varied as the sounds—some pleasant, some unpleasant. Predominant was the odor of fermented fish in the form of a sauce called *nuoc mam*. *Nuoc mam* is to Vietnamese as ketchup is to Americans.

Unless *nuoc mam* is of the highest quality, it smells like rotten fish. It

A *cyclopousse* driver rests in the oppressive midday heat.

is consumed with most foods and at nearly every meal. In his memoir, *A Soldier Reports,* Gen. William Westmoreland told of an experience with which many of us who were in Vietnam can identify: "Kitsy and I both had some difficulty adjusting to Vietnamese food, notably *nuoc mam,* . . . As Kitsy put it you ate it in self defense as the only way to be able to tolerate the odor of it on anyone else. A bottle of *nuoc mam* once broke on my plane, and we almost had to don gas masks in order to survive."*

Nuoc mam combined with odors produced by almost totally inadequate sanitation facilities led to a nearly intolerable situation. The building walls and curbstones were often used as toilets. A common sight was that of a cab driver pulling over, getting out, and urinating on a building or wall. Another frequent spectacle was that of someone defecating freely on a sidewalk or curb. Babies and small children wore no diapers and consequently relieved themselves wherever they stood or sat.

The streets and sidewalks of Saigon were not only the sites of human and animal wastes, they were also spattered and stained red. These stains resembled blood and at first look were disconcerting to me. Actually they were produced by the chewing of betel nut, which is a product of the areca palm. These popular nuts could produce a mild narcotic effect, and they could rot teeth.

With the searing sun beating down upon the walls and sidewalks, frequently decorated with human and animal excreta, much of Saigon took on the odor of an enormous outhouse. And with traffic clogging every street, exhaust fumes reached catastrophic levels.

Not every odor was unpleasant, of course. Lovely Nguyen Hue, the Street of Flowers, was located in Saigon Central. Along this boulevard were kiosks brimming with fragrant blossoms. I recall the masses of rainbow-colored orchids of all types. Richly aromatic gardenias scented the air.

Food aromas were often inviting, wafting from the outdoor cooking that was customary. Peanut sauce and meat cooking made a pleasant combination. Tropical fruits such as papayas, pineapples, mangoes, bananas, sugar apples, and guavas, displayed by hucksters on pony carts, produced a rich mixture of subtle scents.

After absorbing the initial sensations, I began to observe the cultural subtleties. What I found was a city of contrasts, a blend of Oriental—

*Gen. William C. Westmoreland, *A Soldier Reports* (New York: Dell Publishing, 1976), 59.

A land of contrasts: ox carts and Mercedes Benzes, street beggars and the world on the other side of the villa fence

that is, the Chinese-Vietnamese—and Occidental French and other Caucasian groups. East met West in Saigon.

There appeared to be two rather extreme classes of Vietnamese residing in Saigon. The elite class lived in stucco villas built in the French-Colonial style. Many of the villas were enclosed by walls topped with broken glass. An occasional glimpse of the villa grounds revealed the artistry of topiary and lushly manicured tropical gardens. The wealthy traveled in Mercedes sedans or Peugeots. This elite class was comprised of bankers, entrepreneurs, importers, and politicians. They employed the peasants as servants, houseboys, cooks, and nannies.

The peasant class of Saigon lived a spartan existence in homes of corrugated metal, or old packing crates, or perhaps a tenement of stucco, if they were lucky. The children, lacking yards, played in public parks or in the streets. Ramshackle housing hugged the edge of the Saigon River. These hovels were protected by scores of lovely tamarind trees, whose rich, full foliage provided shelter from the scorching sun.

Most often, the Saigon peasants were employed as peddlers, servants, laborers, and stevedores. Favorite modes of transportation were cyclos (short for *cyclopousses*) or bicycles. Friendly people flashed bright pink smiles, their teeth stained by the betel nut they obsessively chewed. The children suffered from serious tooth decay brought on by the incessant chewing and sucking of sugar cane.

Even though there was a middle class, similar to middle-class America and including public servants and shopkeepers, I was struck primarily by the contrasts that grew out of the interaction of the social extremes. At intersections, it was common to see an elegant Mercedes sedan confront a lumbering cart pulled by a team of oxen. Saigon peasants congregated in front of villa walls, talking, begging, chewing betel nut or smoking cigarettes and pipes, and gambling. On the other side of this stucco barrier I imagined a far different existence. I had glimpsed the lush ornamental gardens and further visualized organized households, beautiful bamboo and wicker furnishings, and privileged children playing upon trimmed grass—all in glaring contrast to life on the street side of the wall.

Many streets had names that translated to nicknames—Street of Pets, Street of Leather, Street of Flowers, to name a few. Perhaps the most famous street of all was Duong Tu Do (Liberty Street). It was located in the most fashionable area of downtown Saigon and was lined with fascinating shops and cafés. There, the many tailor and fabric shops specialized in fine brocades, silks, cottons, and synthetics, available in a wide variety of prints and solid colors.

Ready-made clothes were unattainable in Saigon. It was necessary to have everything (except for traditional undergarments) custom-tailored. After selecting material for the garment, the customer sought a reputable tailoring shop that provided fashion books, usually dated. After the customer selected a clothing design, the tailor attempted to duplicate it—without a pattern. Depending upon the tailor's degree of skill, the results fell into one of two categories: attractive or disastrous.

As we explored our new environment, we discovered many delightful sidewalk cafés. These cafés, extensions of established indoor restaurants, sported brightly colored awnings or umbrellas affixed over tables. It was entertaining, after an afternoon of shopping in the hot Central Market, to sit sipping a carbonated orange drink and watch the passersby and the always exciting traffic.

For advice on food selections in the many restaurants, from fancy establishments to ordinary street cafés to "greasy spoons," we relied upon the Saigon veterans or our Vietnamese friends. We constantly plied them with questions about the contents of various dishes. Sometimes I was sorry I asked.

Dog steak! What was it? Filet of Fox Terrier? None of us wanted to imagine it, let alone eat it. Then there was monkey-paw soup, with little paws floating on the surface. Other popular delicacies were goat kidneys and testicles with, for us Americans, fries and slaw on the side. Slightly less repulsive was the roast sparrow—still no takers. A dark, congealed placentalike dish turned out to be duck-blood pudding. It was fare few Western diners could stomach. For those who imbibed, there was a special drink—one could call it a Vietnamese Bloody Mary, since sparrow or snake blood was mixed with rice wine.

Nothing, however, compared to one popular dish: boiled half-hatched duck eggs. They were sold in the cafés or by the street vendors. A small hole was punched into the egg, allowing the juicy contents to drip into the mouth. The egg was then peeled, and a portion of the tiny duck embryo was placed on a spoon, sprinkled with a spicy herb and salt and pepper, and then eaten. To enjoy the eggs to the fullest, one sipped rice wine while consuming them.

As I adapted to life in Saigon, I began to establish certain criteria in the area of food consumption. For the most part I favored eating in quarters or at other BOQs, the USO, and military messes. Any military assignment brings with it restricted freedoms—due to geographical circumstances, security precautions, and so forth—and in Saigon common sense about food and water consumption was a factor. The tap water available publicly was nonpotable. Likewise, food consumed at local restaurants, bars, and clubs was not always prepared hygienically and could therefore be contaminated in any number of ways. And although food was often fresh, it had been raised or grown with the use of "night soil," a fertilizer composed of human excrement. Thus parasites were a major problem. To dine out required some thought and even research.

Still, dining out became a favored pastime and common sense could not always rule. One particular French restaurant offered a great onion soup. The soup was served scorching hot in a crock with thick blobs of melted cheese floating on top. But was it safe to eat? Tweedie and I tempted fate one day. Seated at a table close to the kitchen, we had just about convinced ourselves that the soup was self-sterilized (because it was so hot) when we caught sight of what was going on in the kitchen. Aside from the overall filth, live chickens were running freely about the preparation table. It was a tribute to the chef that we overlooked the unwholesome kitchen and took our chances with his wonderful soup.

Among the nurses, probably Penny was the most adventurous diner. Having arrived in the city five months before we had, she had had more time to become comfortable with the environment—comfortable enough to throw caution to the winds. If she had standards regarding dining out in Saigon, they were not readily apparent to me. Penny would go anywhere and try anything in the city. She was not concerned with amoebic dysentery and never contracted it. This was more a testimony to good luck than to common sense. Practically no one escaped the ailment, even with taking precautions.

As we sat in the pleasant cafés, it was difficult to realize that a shooting war was being fought perhaps five miles away—city noise was so great that gunfire couldn't be heard. But with increasing frequency, the Viet Cong began to target the little cafés, concentrating on those spots popular with Americans. The VC tossed grenades into the midst of café patrons. Another favorite and deadly tactic was to hide a *plastique* bomb somewhere in the establishment. A timer detonated the bomb, often when the café was filled with people.

Eventually, these acts of violence forced café owners to move their businesses indoors. Many owners installed ugly steel mesh to protect their customers from thrown grenades. It was a shame to see favorite outdoor spots disappear. They had added so much to the ambience of the city.

The less elegant side streets of Saigon presented a different atmosphere. In many ways they were the most interesting to explore and observe. The lower-class way of life in the Orient is to live in public. Privacy, it seemed, was without meaning.

Each day, from noon until three o'clock, people simply found a comfortable spot along the street and lay down for the equivalent of a Mexican siesta. I watched young girls on curbstones comb lice from each other's hair. Games of chance were played by groups of boys and men. Players would squat on the sidewalks, deeply engrossed in the progress of the game. Nearby, boys would pitch one-dong coins at cracks in the sidewalk.

Informal "offices" sprouted along the side streets. The dentist's office consisted of a low wooden box. A jar of teeth, evidence of his skill, was prominently displayed alongside his extractors. The patient sat on the box while this primitive practitioner pulled the offending molar. This procedure was undertaken sans anesthesia.

The barber, too, operated a makeshift shop, propping his mirror against a fence or wall. His client would take a seat on a box or stool, and in minutes the hair was skillfully cut. After a liberal application of lavender-scented hair oil, the freshly coiffed customer was ready to go.

Not far away, bloody slabs of freshly killed meat lay on the sidewalk. After the customer made his selection, the butcher cleaved the desired cut from the bloody stack, wrapped it in banana leaves or newspaper, and tied it with a handle for carrying. Often, wrapping was not available or desired. A common sight was that of a customer pedaling away from the butcher's with a naked chunk of meat or fish swaying from the handlebars.

On a nearby corner stood an impromptu bicycle service station. The mechanic, who specialized in tire repairs, operated a no-frills business. On the pavement sat a tub of water, tube-patching material, and a pump. If only air was required, the charge was one dong (less than one cent). Since my bike never experienced a flat tire, I never learned the cost of a repair.

As a nurse, I was curious about the Oriental apothecary shops.

On the sidewalks of Saigon: a barber, a medicine man, and the "Good Humor Man," who crushed sugar cane for sweets

These quaint and tiny shops were located throughout the city. The small front room of such a shop contained one or two large trunks housing dozens of small drawers in which medicines of all kinds were kept. I noted a sort of chopper/grater, a heavy mortar and pestle, and a cast-iron grinder displayed on a counter. These items, plus an abacus, constituted a fully equipped *pharmacie*.

The druggists I encountered were usually old men, small and wizened with delicate, wispy goatees, and long, long mandarin-style fingernails. The trunk drawers contained hundreds of folk remedies, largely consisting of assorted herbs, roots, flowers, and bark. There were also exotic medicaments such as powdered rhinoceros horn, dried powdered snakes, frogs, pig entrails, and animal foeti. Later in my stay, I worked with a gifted Vietnamese ophthalmologist who shared with me the identities of these strange substances. Through further study, I learned that these preparations were to be taken along with special diets, because it was believed that the effectiveness of the medication was either enhanced or diminished by certain foods.

The Vietnamese ophthalmologist also told me that the Oriental druggists never modernized or improved their techniques. In the 1960s, Saigon medicines were prescribed in precisely the same manner as they had been centuries earlier.

Watching a diagnosis as it was being made by the druggist fascinated those of us who follow the tenets of Western medicine. The druggist pinched or pummeled the individual at the focal point of his pain. He frequently examined the skin or looked at the tongue. Having arrived at his diagnosis, he set about preparing the suitable remedies, mixing some of the contents of the medicine drawers in the mortar. He might take a piece of some unidentifiable material and pulverize it in the grinder.

When the medicines were concocted, he placed them in tiny packets of rice paper. He then delivered a lecture to his customer, presumably discussing the directions for use of the medicines and perhaps giving some additional advice regarding proper diet. After a couple of quick clicks of the abacus beads, the patron settled his account and was on his way.

Many streets we traveled led to the Saigon River. Because I had an affection for all that was nautical, the river held a special fascination for me. I made it my goal to explore as many facets of the waterfront as possible and became especially interested in the Saigon River people.

While Saigon is primarily Vietnamese, its twin city, Cholon, is predominantly Chinese. Both Saigon and Cholon lie about fifty miles inland from the South China Sea, up the navigable Saigon River. Because the river is their common waterway, they share the special culture of the boat people.

The river traffic consisted of oceangoing vessels and Vietnamese and U.S. warships as well as small sampans and junks, the skiffs and sailboats of the Orient. Water traffic, like its city counterpart, was heavy and noisy. Boy, was it noisy! Radios blared, people shouted, horns blasted, animals squealed and squawked, firecrackers popped.

Sampans were more than just homes or workplaces for the river people. The complete cycle of life—birth, growth, education, maturity, and death—unfolded aboard these remarkable vessels.

They were of every size, averaging twenty to thirty feet in overall length. Constructed primarily of oak or mahogany, some sampans were engine-powered while others were propelled by their occupants using poles. Their thatched roofs provided protection from the monsoon rains and brutal sun. Hulls were usually unpainted with the exception of colorful eyes, one eye painted on either side of the bow. It was believed that these eyes warded off evil spirits.

The chief source of income for river merchants was transporting produce (such as rice, fruits, vegetables) and other goods (lumber, pipe, baskets). The decks of the sampans were crowded with cargo and livestock of all descriptions, either contained in big cages or running freely. Sometimes, on the fantail, several small, squealing pigs would be scampering in every direction.

The boat people's lifestyle was at the very least devoid of any sort of amenities. Rarely was a sampan seen without laundry drying on bamboo poles. Meals were foods such as rice, fish, and tea, cooked over a tiny charcoal brazier. The muddy Saigon River provided water to cook with, dip your toothbrush in, and use for the family's laundry.

The river also served as a community toilet, and garbage was dumped over the side of the boats. Imagine washing yourself or drinking tea made from such water. Dishes were washed by swishing them in the polluted waters. The Saigon River was infested with all kinds of floating debris, including dead animals, snakes, rotting garbage, and dead fish.

This lifestyle probably remains unchanged. As I found true of so many of the Eastern ways—such as the street *pharmacies,* which were never improved or modernized—the river people were like relics of the past existing in the present.

The present for Saigon, however, was troubled by hostilities. Engagement with the "irregular," nonuniformed troops of the VC increased. Saigon itself was becoming a field of battle.

SIX

City in Chaos

CHAOS WAS EPIDEMIC in Saigon. Countless volumes on Vietnam's socioeconomic, political, and military history describe the heightening tensions. Suffice it to say that in 1963, the region was a volatile mix of opposing interests, power struggles, and political intrigue. The acts of terrorism concerned me most. By October 1963, Viet Cong terrorist strikes were almost daily events in the city—events that the staff at Duong Duong had to contend with.

Within five days of our arrival, we observed a terrorist attack. Flo, Tweedie, and I had just arrived at our quarters when an explosion rattled the windows. Rushing to our balcony, we took in a scene of utter confusion. Five bleeding bodies were strewn in an area outside the entrance to the Central Market. One was that of a child. We learned later that an explosive charge had been planted in a vendor's fruit basket.

This war had no rules. Civilians and military personnel far from the fields of conventional battle were fair game. Apprehension of a suspect was difficult, since the ensuing confusion caused by the bomb or grenade served as a cover to enable the terrorist to fade into the crowd, becoming indistinguishable. Suddenly, we understood the briefing officer's warning—avoid mingling with street crowds. General Timmes had told us that it would be impossible to differentiate between a Viet Cong terrorist and a "friendly" unless he shot at you. In that case, he said, there would be little doubt. Danger, I realized, was indeed everywhere.

The evening after the Central Market bomb, Tweedie and I decided to go to the movies—but then we discovered that we had already seen the film. Instead, we stayed at home. Around 1900, the city was jolted by a powerful explosion. From the balcony, we watched the activity below. A dense black mushroom of smoke arose from the area of town where the cinema was located. Capitol Kinh Do Theatre, where English-language films were shown, had been bombed, suffering minor damage. Homes nearby were destroyed, and one Vietnamese woman was injured. Tweedie and I had been lucky. This time no Americans were harmed. The next time the theater was targeted by terrorists, American casualties would be high.

I recall vividly when a terrorist strike brought victims to Duong Duong for the first time. Pershing Field was a recreational area located near downtown Saigon. Various military units used the field for softball and other sports. Sometime prior to that evening's softball game, bombs were buried beneath the bleachers. They were detonated electrically, when a telephone receiver located in a nearby phone booth was lifted at a predesignated time. Not all the bombs detonated, but enough damage was done to kill three people, injure twenty-three, and hospitalize seven. At Duong Duong we responded quickly, attending to shrapnel wounds, lacerations, contusions, and fractures.

We were all aware that Viet Cong activities were becoming more sophisticated. As a result, we knew that more terrorist victims—war casualties of a different kind—would need emergency treatment. These patients often presented themselves when least expected. Unlike casualties from the battlefield, where a phone call would alert us to incoming ambulances and "dust-offs" (helicopter medevacs), there was virtually no forewarning.

Such was the case one Saturday night when I received several wounded GIs, victims of a "shoe box" bomb, a *plastique* explosive hidden in a paper-wrapped box. They were enjoying off-duty time in a Saigon bar popular with Americans when the incident occurred.

The first casualty arrived in a moribund state. I have never witnessed greater destruction of a human body, except, perhaps, in the case of airplane crash victims. Within ten minutes of arrival, he died. He had sustained maximum facial and neck damage, both arms had been blown off, one hip had been completely disarticulated, and there had been associated massive destruction of all the major vessels in the femoral area. Besides the blast injuries, he suffered major flash burns from exploding *plastique*.

Three more casualties followed. One soldier suffered severe head trauma; the second had profuse bleeding caused by damage to major blood vessels located in the upper arm; the third sustained thirty-five

Terrorists bombed this bar, which was frequented by GIs.

shrapnel wounds, extending from the back of his head to his heels.

We spent that Saturday night in the Operating Room. The OR filled with the sounds of clicking instruments, the gurgling of the wound-suction machine, the metallic clanking noise of a wrench manipulating oxygen-tank valves, the rhythmic sound of a patient breathing into the rebreathing bag attached to the anesthesia machine, and the subdued voices of the OR team—Walt Johnson, Tweedie, the corpsmen, and myself. At 0800, we put in the final suture and dressed the last wound.

Later in the morning, one of the demolition officers assigned to investigate the incident offered the details of the explosion. The soldier who died had noticed a package on a window ledge in the bar. He suspected it to be a shoe-box bomb. Picking it up, he examined it and then tossed it into the alley outside. Nothing happened. Then he left the bar and picked up the box again. This time it exploded in his hands.

We learned that the soldier's judgment was impaired as a result of a heavy intake of *Ba Muoi Ba,* a Vietnamese beer. How ironic the situation was. His military occupation specialty was demolition expert. His training and instincts, impaired by alcohol, had failed him when they had been most needed.

Occasionally, MAAG headquarters received a tip-off of a planned terrorist strike. A short time after the Pershing Field bombing, we received such a warning. A reliable Vietnamese informant told MAAG that our hospital was targeted. I was on duty, working the evening shift, and suddenly I found myself charged with the responsibility of securing the hospital from a terrorist strike.

In less than an hour after the phone call from headquarters, a company of ARVN troops encircled the compound. All outside lights were turned on. Both gates were closed and barred. Window shutters were secured, and I ordered all hands off the balconies. If an attack had been planned for that night, it never came. It was most likely successfully deterred.

Many nights, we could both see and hear strikes on villages outside the city. Less than five miles away, an orange muzzle flash—brilliant color against the endless black sky—preceded the blast of exploding howitzer shells. Then the blackness was erased entirely by the dazzling brightness of magnesium flares. There was a certain sense of unreality in reading about the fighting we observed at night in the following morning's paper. Instantaneous reporting had documented or codified images still vivid in our minds.

We heard the distinctive crackle of small-arms fire day and night. Our own hospital compound was alive with gunfire one day when a tower guard spotted a suspected terrorist on a nearby rooftop and fired at him.

Within weeks of my arrival in Saigon, I was exposed to all kinds of war-related violence. It seemed that any manner of bizarre gunplay could occur. While I was returning from evening duty one night, a Vietnamese policeman fired his .38-caliber revolver across the hood of my car in an effort to stop a man fleeing down the street. After that episode,

A Buddhist monk making the ultimate sacrifice in the name of religious protest

I began to carry with me a .22-caliber pistol whenever I had P.M. duty.

Besides the chaos imposed by terrorist activity, other turmoil unfolded. On Saturday, 5 October 1963, I witnessed perhaps the supreme form of religious protest. I had been viewing the street scene from my quarters when a taxi pulled curbside and from it emerged a Buddhist monk dressed in traditional saffron-colored robes and carrying a can. He did not hesitate; he proceeded to a spot on the sidewalk and sat down. Pouring the contents of the can over his robes, he struck a match and was immediately engulfed in flames. Even though other monk burnings had occurred, I still couldn't believe what I was witnessing. I called to Flo and Tweedie to join me. A crowd gathered, growing larger and larger as the monk was incinerated.

I went for my camera and took several shots of the crowd, with the monk the focal point. The monk flamed, arms upraised rigidly, then tumbled over on his side. Still smoldering, he was blackened, totally burned. The stench of charred flesh wafted upward. By now probably more than a thousand people had joined the onlookers.

Suddenly, there was a disturbance from within the crowd. We saw three individuals being beaten. A fire engine, siren screaming, arrived. Firemen hosed down the monk, who was then unceremoniously tossed inside a police ambulance. Police cars converged on the scene, and the officers attempted to disperse the crowd. Shortly after, two truckloads of ARVN soldiers arrived and cordoned off the area. I continued to snap photos as we waited to see what would happen. Martial law was effected briefly, and within thirty minutes from the time the monk had stepped from his taxi, order had been restored. It was almost as though nothing had happened.

Later I left for P.M. duty. Arriving at 1500, I obtained the report on the patients from the A.M. nurse, then responded to a call to go directly to the Emergency Room, where a civilian with a head injury was arriving.

He was conscious, bleeding from a five-inch scalp laceration and probably suffering a concussion. After skull X-rays were taken, we cleaned and sutured the wound. He was then moved to a ward bed. During the admission process, I discovered that this patient was John Sharkey of NBC News. Sharkey told me that he, along with two other war correspondents, was covering a monk immolation in the park adjacent to the Central Market. They arrived at the park after receiving a tip-off phone call that an event would take place at about noon near Le Loi Street. They were walking up Le Loi when they noticed the smoke and hastened to the park.

The scuffle that I observed from the balcony was the trio being pistol-whipped by, Sharkey believed, members of the Saigon government's secret police force. I wondered if the secret police had been tipped off as well, perhaps waiting for the three American journalists to arrive. As the three attempted to photograph the immolation, the secret police interfered and ordered the journalists to turn over their equipment. When the men refused, they were beaten and the equipment confiscated; the film was destroyed.

I told Sharkey that I had witnessed the entire incident and also had taken some photographs. This information interested the reporter, who was concerned that trumped-up assault charges might result from the altercation. He asked me to hold onto my film; if charges were pressed, Sharkey hoped that something in the photographs would reveal the true nature of the attack.

Martial law was implemented often and proved effective in terms of restoring temporary order. And after awhile I began to note a subtle shift—the abnormal was becoming normal. The unexpected became the expected. All of us began to adapt.

Saigon, however, became an increasingly hazardous duty station. Eventually, it became known as Bombsville to those in the military stationed outside the city. Personnel on R and R (rest and rehabilitation leave) preferred to visit other locations—anywhere but unstable Saigon. Some soldiers I met said they found it safer to be on duty in the Mekong Delta.

Events were breaking around me so quickly that there was scarcely enough time to react. At this pace, I wondered how long I could remain on the edge. Nothing in my nursing career or my Korean War duty had prepared me for Saigon, where the limits of my endurance were tested. We eventually adapted as the citizens of the city had, by taking events in stride, by viewing the extraordinary as ordinary. Because for all of us, adapting became the key to survival.

By the beginning of October 1963, we had been in country for three weeks. Because of the growing instability, all military personnel were given a five-mile perimeter and told not to exceed it. The constant threat of terrorist activities only compounded the situation. For the first time, I felt claustrophobia. It was time to get away—even for a weekend. On 12 October, Tweedie and I received permission to exceed the perimeter. We were granted our first liberty weekend since coming to Vietnam: we would travel 200 miles north to Da Lat. Miss Ninh, our switchboard operator, volunteered to be our guide.

SEVEN
Liberty and Diversion

IT WAS 12 OCTOBER 1963. The Douglas DC-3 descended through puffy, white, cotton-ball clouds. Below me lay an unspoiled landscape. The rugged mountain terrain of the Central Highlands was spiked by miles of lofty pine trees. Cut into the valley floor was the single airstrip that served the city of Da Lat. The French had designed Da Lat to resemble an Alpine resort. There were mountains, a large artificial lake, waterfalls, forests, hotels, and impressive villas.

Instead of the oppressive heat and humidity that greeted us as we stepped off the plane in Saigon, the mountain air was cool, crisp, and refreshing. Tweedie, Ninh, and I were met by Ninh's cousin Xuyen, a friendly man who spoke no English. We traveled thirty minutes through countryside marked by brillant colors. Red poinsettias, massed in fields, reminded me that Da Lat was the unofficial flower capital of South Vietnam. I had read that a greenhouse industry flourished. Fifteen hundred varieties of orchids were bred as well as dozens of other tropical flowers.

The bright red was set off by vivid green rice paddies and forests of dark green pines. Giant water buffalo were urged along the shoulder of the narrow asphalt road by diminutive mountain tribesmen, the Montagnards. Da Lat's rainy season was ending. The entire scene was sunwashed and sparkling. And it was quiet. Unlike the outskirts of Saigon, the approach to Da Lat was blissfully devoid of commotion, congestion, and noise.

We arrived at the Da Lat Palace on Yersin Street, where we had overnight reservations. There was a brief verbal commotion at the front desk, Ninh's conversation becoming animated. We learned that our res-

ervations had not been held, and so we had to make our way across the
town square to the Da Lat Hotel. It was less impressive than the Palace
and reminded Tweedie and me, all too clearly, of the Majestic Hotel in
Saigon.

Our rooms were furnished with Gothic teak and mahogany pieces.
Above our beds, soiled mosquito netting, dusty and yellowed with age,
was rolled up over the bed posters. The nets were so ancient and brittle
that they crumbled in our hands. We decided that we would rather take
our chances with the mosquitoes.

An hour later, Ninh and Xuyen arrived to take us sightseeing. Neither Tweedie nor I were prepared for the utter tranquillity of Da Lat.
Gone were the rumbling explosions, the crackle of small-arms fire, the
scream of sirens, the frenetic urgency of the hospital routine. I didn't
notice street vendors or their musical language. Even the pace was
stately compared with bustling Saigon. People moved slowly. The
streets seemed almost deserted; there were no congested boulevards.
Da Lat was a serene oasis in the midst of battle-torn South Vietnam.

When Ninh and Xuyen announced that they would be taking us on a
picnic, Tweedie and I knew we had a problem. In the month since our
arrival in Vietnam, I'd been sampling some of the cuisine and was not
too fond of it. I was famished, but chilled at the thought of *nuoc mam*-
soaked delicacies. Ninh and Xuyen were our hosts, however, and had
generously offered their time for sightseeing and thoughtfully preparing
a picnic.

The trip in Xuyen's aged Peugeot took us far into the Annamite
Mountains, until we arrived at a picturesque spot in a park-like area.
Along the way we had been treated to a sweeping panorama of the
mountains and the valleys below, where produce farms spread over
acres of rich land. There had been little conversation; we were too engrossed in watching the scenery to chat.

A picnic table was shaded from the sun by a thatched roof woven
from nipa palm. We were at the base of the Prenn Waterfall, which tumbled noisily a short distance away. On the other side of the picnic grove,
there was lush, green jungle.

Ninh spread the lunch items on the table. I breathed a sigh of relief.
No *nuoc mam*. She had brought bottles of warm coke, bananas, and a loaf
of French bread. There were a few unidentifiable dishes, one resembling
Spam. Not wanting to offend Ninh or Xuyen, we took generous help-
ings. Every once in awhile I caught Tweedie slipping something into her
napkin. I tossed some of the food I did not trust into the jungle when I

Vistas of fertile valleys made for refreshing sights.

had the chance. Later both Tweedie and I confessed to feeling guilty about disposing of so much of Ninh's picnic.

Following our meal, Ninh took us farther into the country, nearly an hour's drive, to the home of her sister. The home was a modest wooden frame dwelling and well kept. Ninh's brother-in-law opened a special bottle of fig brandy, which we sampled. Conversation was awkward, since the couple did not know English. But they were gracious hosts, and we enjoyed our brief stop.

It was by now midafternoon. We arrived at the edge of a dense wood. A short distance away stood a magnificent old Buddhist pagoda. We removed our shoes out of respect, as is customary, and entered through huge, solid teak doors that had been unlocked by a monk Ninh located. Incense in the form of joss sticks burned, creating a smoky, aromatic atmosphere. The structures within the pagoda—the altars and benches—were handsomely carved. The altar was particularly ornate, with rich, intricate features.

Taking to the road again, we traveled deeper into the countryside.

The narrow route was winding through hills and woods and jungles. Suddenly, I had a choice photo opportunity. A herd of water buffalo grazed beside a stream. Grabbing my camera, I approached the docile beasts. Face to face with a particularly old bull, I photographed while he flapped his big ears, chewed his cud, and belched loudly.

On another stop we followed a trail into the jungle, where I encountered an elephant. He was ancient and elegant, absolutely huge. Missing a tusk, he was quite a sight as he chewed on sugar-cane stalks. At times he swayed from side to side, blowing dirt over his shoulder to rid himself of small, black, pesky flies.

Ninh insisted that we travel still further away from Da Lat and into the hinterlands. For the first time, I was uneasy. I questioned Ninh about Viet Cong activities in the area, and she assured me that we were safe. Still, I grew concerned. American medical personnel might be particularly desirable to the VC. Dr. Patricia Smith, an American civilian doctor, had been captured shortly after our arrival. (She was still in captivity a year later.)

Ninh and Xuyen located another beautiful spot. In the distance, we could hear a waterfall. A steep trail descended to the pool below. I ventured down to explore for a moment, the others remaining behind. The

Lovely areas (here, Prenn Falls) could be bloody battlegrounds.

pool was sparkling and crystal clear. The late-afternoon sun slanted through masses of vegetation and trees. In the clearing, beside a swiftly moving stream a short distance from the pool, something glinted in the half-light.

There were hundreds of spent shells scattered about the clearing. I scooped up a few M-1 rifle cartridge cases and other .30-caliber shells. They had been fired recently. Some of the shells were not expended, their casings shiny and new. Tree branches and limbs were snapped, the area trampled down. The soft dirt still showed evidence of footprints. I moved quickly, climbing the steep trail in record time. "*Di di mau,* let's go." I didn't offer an explanation, since I didn't want to alarm our party. It was getting late, the countryside was lonely, and I had just discovered the remnants of a recent firefight. It didn't help that as we drove down the road, we passed a large troop convoy. The ARVN soldiers were outfitted in full battle dress.

Night fell quickly and brought with it a heightened sense of anxiety. There was a saying in Vietnam: the night belongs to the Viet Cong. After about an hour, we could see the lights of Da Lat in the distance. We had not encountered any roadblocks and the region remained quiet and undisturbed. I arrived at our hotel greatly relieved.

It was Saturday night, and Tweedie and I decided to dine at the MAAG mess in town. Ninh, however, surprised us with a dinner invitation, and we had no choice but to accept it.

Our soap, a real luxury in Vietnam, was missing from our rooms. We did our best to clean up before setting out on the three-mile walk to Ninh's residence, stopping at a rustic drugstore and purchasing a chocolate bar to snack on later. We shivered in the cold air, a far cry from the thick, hot Saigon nights, and longed to return to Bombsville for a reliable meal. We were that hungry!

We found the family's home without difficulty. It was located above their radio-repair shop in west Da Lat. We were greeted at the head of a steep, narrow staircase and entered the living room. Ninh's mother arrived after we had been seated. She was striking in a dark brown robe with mandarin collar and black headdress, typical of the old traditional Tonkinese dress. When she smiled, I noted evidence of a decades-old Vietnamese custom, one intended to suggest beauty and a wealthy station in life. Her teeth had been painted coal black!

Tea was served and came in an unending supply to be poured steaming hot into tiny, white china cups. I was reminded that Ninh's family at one time engaged in tea-growing on a plantation in Hanoi. Ninh explained that when Vietnam was divided in 1954, her family fled south and left behind all landholdings and possessions. They arrived in Da Lat stripped of their fortune and intent on reestablishing the family income.

Dinner was announced by the maid, and we were seated among Ninh's curious relatives. I cringed when the first dish arrived. It was an enormous fish cooked intact and accompanied by dishes of *nuoc mam*. Its shriveled eyes stared blankly at Tweedie, who in turn lost her appetite.

After dinner we said our thank yous (*Cam on ong*) and good-byes (*Chau ong*) and nearly sprinted back to the hotel. We had had all the beauty and tranquillity we could handle in one weekend.

Our Da Lat liberty was both frustrating and fascinating. Without Ninh's guidance we wouldn't have had the opportunity to tour the region, but Ninh had underestimated the potential danger, evidence of which I discovered by the waterfall. And we realized that travel held terrors of another kind. We had consumed small quantities of the foods prepared for us and had courted hepatitis, amebiasis, and other intestinal parasites. The incubation period was forty days. Neither of us could afford to get sick. It would be a very long forty days.

I encountered Captain Gens on Monday morning. He asked about the trip, and I gave him a brief description of the highlights. Suddenly the captain became agitated. I had been describing the waterfall discovery when he threw his hands up in despair and sternly informed me of the facts as he saw them. The Viet Cong, he explained, made frequent trips into Da Lat to purchase supplies. Had we been captured, Captain Gens said, he would have had a real international incident on his hands. That was all I needed to hear. For the foreseeable future, I would try to find interesting recreation in Saigon.

Anyone who has served in the military knows the importance of off-duty time. In Saigon it was an absolute necessity. Free time served to help us relax, encouraged us to socialize, and enabled us to retain a healthy perspective. Unlike out-of-country R and R leave, off-duty time had to be incorporated into our daily lives and into the reality of Saigon. While I was stationed on Adak Island in the Aleutians, our restriction of freedom was imposed by the geography. Adak was tiny and isolated. In Saigon the restriction was different. Saigon was unpredictable and, to a degree, unsafe. These circumstances dictated certain constraints. Establishing a social life and routine that adhered to military policy and provided balance for personnel became a challenge.

I learned from Penny and Flo that the Cercle Sportif Saigonnais and the Club Nautique had much to offer in the way of physical recreation. I applied for membership at the Cercle on Hong Thap Tu Street, just a short bike ride away from my quarters. The Cercle was housed in a sprawling, handsome French colonial–style structure. Cool, shady verandas overlooked sumptuous grounds, tennis courts, and the pool. I would frequently cycle over to the Cercle during my free mornings and, if I could find a partner, would play a set or two of tennis, swim a few laps, and have lunch.

Henry Cabot Lodge was the American ambassador to Vietnam during most of my tour of duty in Saigon. Ambassador Lodge and his gracious wife, Emily, had also joined the Cercle, since the official residence had no recreational amenities.

Shortly after the Lodges had arrived in country, Mrs. Lodge had begun to organize welcome teas for women—embassy personnel, military wives, nurses, or others in the country on official government business. I attended one such tea, met the Lodges, and became friends with them and later with their niece Emily. A recent graduate of Radcliffe, she arrived from the States for a brief visit and soon after contracted amebiasis. I got to know her when she came to Duong Duong for several days' treatment, and following her recovery we would meet at the Cercle Sportif for a swim and tennis.

I enjoyed the Lodges immensely. They were friendly and without airs. Our conversations were not particularly political; more often than not we talked about the importance of physical fitness or the beauty of the country, or perhaps news from home. On one occasion, Mrs. Lodge told me that the ambassador had been distressed at the severity of the wounds he had observed during one of his frequent visits to patients in Duong Duong.

The Club Nautique was a boating and water-ski club located at the foot of Ham Nghi Street. Its outstanding feature was a delightful riverfront deck where al fresco dining was enjoyed. The U.S. Navy had been granted privileges there. From the deck, the city of Khan Hoi was visible on the far shore. I remember the tiny thatched-roof huts built on pilings and sprinkled along the shoreline. Beyond the village stretched miles of lush tropical foliage. During the day it was an idyllic sight, like a scene from *Robinson Crusoe,* but after dark it harbored danger.

At night Khan Hoi was off limits to military personnel. The Viet Cong prowled the city and surrounding villages, and there had been episodes of sniper activity, village fighting, and attacks on Americans.

One sniper attack occurred in broad daylight. An American, perhaps a civilian, had been waterskiing, and a sniper opened fire. Fortunately, the skier was not hit.

A more pleasant memory is that of the spectacular sunsets I observed from the Club Nautique porch. The sunsets were brilliant in their myriad colors. Since twilight is nearly absent in the balmy tropics, the city was, with the last rays of sun, immediately wrapped in a soft darkness.

Leisure was otherwise found at the American-run Kinh Do Theatre, even if we saw films that had been released at least a year earlier in the States. Once, we attended a Vietnamese screening of an American film starring Marshall Thompson (still sometimes seen on cable television) and a beautiful Vietnamese starlet who, when she wasn't acting, was employed by the Navy at HedSuppAct—an interesting bit of movie trivia. That screening was unusual because both Chinese and Vietnamese subtitles appeared on both sides of the screen, providing more than a comfortable level of distraction.

And the Saigon Zoo on Thong Nhut Street was a cab ride away. A picturesque canal divided the zoo grounds, where the animal habitats were not quite as well designed as their American counterparts but where the botanical gardens were exotic and a feast for the senses.

Extension courses were available through the University of Maryland, and for a brief time I enrolled in a French course. There were various clubs and organizations—Penny became a member of the Vietnamese-American Association, a cultural exchange group that featured learning crafts and listening to poetry and music.

Saigon was, above all, a shopper's paradise. Brass products, woven wicker, bamboo, and half-round baskets, traditionally carried on shoulder-borne poles to transport ducks, stocked the many venues as souvenirs. There was gold and precious-gem jewelry. Fabrics, leather, animals—even sex—were popular commodities. And there was a booming black market where soap, cosmetics, radios, cameras, and cigarettes, all stolen from American facilities, could be found. Almost anything, including pornographic material ("Hey, GI, postcards!"), could be bartered for in the city.

It may seem risky to have been waterskiing, shopping, or sightseeing in Saigon. Nevertheless, none of us could spend our entire tour of duty sheltered in our quarters or at the hospital. Some risks had to be taken, and I never regretted taking them. Despite the difficulty of serving in Vietnam, there was much that alleviated the intensity of hospital duty. Despite everything that this strange and worsening war presented, we, like the South Vietnamese for whom war had been a part of everyday life for many years, adapted.

EIGHT
Coup d'Etat

AMONG OTHER THINGS, my time in Vietnam confirmed the truth in the saying "everything's relative." We had returned from Da Lat to the "safety" of Saigon; despite violent terrorist episodes, Saigon was in our view a relatively safe haven. But so much was happening. It was an inescapable fact that the illusion of safety was dissolving into a different, starker reality. Saigon continued to develop into a full-scale battle zone.

I was writing frequently to my parents, sending off detailed accounts of events as they unfolded. Additionally, I recorded audio tapes to provide me with an oral history of my Vietnam duty. I still have the letters, but I can no longer account for the tapes.

From a 1948 killer hurricane in Key West, Florida, to the events of the Korean airlift, to the violent volcanic eruptions in 1960 near Adak in the Aleutian Islands, I had recorded the dramatic peaks of my career. But these events were about to take second seat to those of 1 November 1963, Saigon, Republic of South Vietnam. The Diem government was about to become history. I was to witness a coup d'état and nearly lose my own life in the process.

On 1 November all of us except for Elaine were scheduled for duty, most of us going on the A.M. shift. The morning had proceeded uneventfully. In fact, my own patient load was somewhat diminished. I recall that I had six patients at the time, no one requiring acute care. My senior hospital corpsman, Paul Burns ("Burnie"), and I had the unit squared away.

At about noon, a hospital visitor told me that he'd heard that the Vietnamese CNO (chief of naval operations) had been assassinated. Rumors of this nature had begun to circulate after the Vietnamese Independence Day parade several weeks earlier. The word in Saigon was that a coup was to be attempted. An effort to oust the Diem government was in the works. Sides would be taken. Those in support of the Diem government remained "loyalists." Those South Vietnamese who favored change and an easing of the oppression imposed by the Diem government became the "rebels."

The assassination rumor proved true. When the Vietnamese CNO was offered the opportunity to join the coup but declined, his aide shot him. The civil war battle lines were drawn. Although we in the hospital community were not aware of it at the time, the complex machinery needed to execute an overthrow of the nation's ruling body was carefully oiled and someone had pushed the button.

A complex tunnel network existed in Vietnam, as described vividly in *The Tunnels of Cu Chi*, by Tom Mangold and John Penycate. As the world later learned, some of the oldest of these tunnels, possibly built during the French colonial era, were accessed by two escaping members of the Diem family. Ngo Dinh Diem, the threatened president, and his brother Ngo Dinh Nhu attempted to vacate the presidential palace. They surfaced over five miles away in Cholon at the home of a Chinese friend. (By Sunday night they were captured, tortured, and assassinated.)

At 1230, a hospital corpsman returning from Cholon brought more news. He had seen barbed-wire barricades and machine-gun emplacements, armed troops, tanks, and armored cars located at intersections along Tran Hung Dao, the main artery linking Saigon and Cholon, and the street on which Duong Duong was located.

As soon as the corpsman finished his story, I walked out onto the street and looked in the direction of Cholon. Only a hundred yards from me I saw a gun emplacement and barbed-wire barricades. Sandbags surrounded the emplacement, and I found myself staring into the barrels of guns pointing directly at me. Troops were working quickly setting up more concertinas, sandbags, and guns. It was siesta time in the city, and so the street, baking in the afternoon sun, was at that moment quiet save for the troop activity. The traffic artery was under the troops' control. It seemed to me that the rumored coup was about to begin—or, perhaps more correctly, had already begun.

Small police stations surrounded Duong Duong. I knew that a coup attempt would lead to a neutralizing of the National Police Force. Duong Duong, I therefore realized, stood a good chance of being caught in the cross fire. Returning to my unit, I let Burnie know I would be upstairs if anyone needed me. Suddenly, gunfire erupted. From the ICU window,

Burnie and I observed one of our gate guards strip to his skivvies, desert his post, and sprint off at high speed, disappearing around the corner of the outpatient building across the street. I ran up the five flights of steps to the top-floor balcony of the hospital. Alone, I looked out over the balustrade and had an excellent view of a city about to explode.

Swarms of bullets flew down the street. Everywhere I looked, I saw tree limbs snapping and flying in all directions. Lead was ricocheting off building walls. People were taking cover in doorways, while others braved exposed balconies and rooftops. If a volley came too close, they scrambled for cover. When the bullets moved out of their immediate range, once again heads popped up.

One of the male staff members joined me on the balcony. The surrounding balustrade was waist-high. As we stood watching the activity, a bullet hit the wall directly in front of us—just three inches from the top of the balustrade. Bits of stucco and dust sprayed the fronts of our uniforms. We dove for cover, crawled inside, and hid under a desk. The enormity of that single shot did not elude us. Either of us could have sustained a fatal injury. Had it struck three inches higher, one of us could have suffered a high abdominal or a low chest wound. If the heart, liver, spleen, stomach, or major vessels had been penetrated by the bullet, the wound could have been life-threatening. We agreed that at least we were in the best place to be—the hospital.

After a few moments, we emerged from under the desk. A corpsman appeared and held out his hand. In his palm lay an expended bullet. He told us that it had penetrated a third-floor wall, falling at a patient's feet. When the patient reached for it, the bullet was still hot. The three of us returned to the balcony. The firing was still in progress. I looked down and saw a bullet. The tip was bent upward slightly. Since it was the only bullet found on the balcony, I realized that it was probably the one that had struck the balustrade. I still have that reminder of a close call.

A soldier in fatigues appeared. Carrying a field radio unit, he explained that he was going to establish communication on a network that would be linked to MAAG headquarters. He turned on the unit and it crackled to life.

The four of us listened intently. For the last fifteen minutes, the shooting in the streets had been steadily escalating. No one suggested that I leave the balcony for safety's sake, and I was just as glad. For the most part we stayed low to the deck, crouched down or stooping. The soldier manipulated the radio. There was a lot of static, but we could hear other radio operators linking up and, occasionally, someone speak-

The coup's prime target: the presidential palace

ing from headquarters. Information pertaining to the coup was fragmented and vague. I wasn't sure who was doing what or where they
were doing it.

The noise from the street fighting eventually gave way to the booming explosions of aircraft rockets. American-made T-28 fighter bombers

Outside the palace guards' barracks: a statue of the deposed Diem and evidence of the volume of gunfire

moved in from the south, swooping low over the presidential palace. Green tracers fired from .50-caliber machine guns streaked the horizon. The palace responded with a return of antiaircraft fire, creating black smoke that arose in puffs and spread out against the deep blue sky.

We watched as the T-28s came in low and fired on the palace, then

The War Room at the presidential palace

pulling up in steep, climbing turns before descending for another pass. After one of the passes we saw an aircraft react as though it had been hit, falling off into a near-vertical dive before disappearing below the tree line. Because the sky was by now filled with smoke, I couldn't be certain but thought the plane had crashed into downtown Saigon. Later I learned that the pilot had taken evasive action from the heavy flak and headed back to Tan Son Nhut.

The scene was surrealistic, the illusion of relative safety totally shattered. This was something out of a movie or a book, I thought. It took a few moments for me to adjust to the reality. Saigon was in turmoil. Thunderous booms rolled across the city. Rapid gunfire peppered buildings, vehicles, and people. The noise was incredible. Still there was no real information coming from the radio.

I was not worried about my unit. My corpsman knew where I was, and I knew that I would be contacted if any emergencies arose. For the present, I wanted to remain on the balcony. When the street fire subsided I decided to have a look. A small black Peugeot, moving slowly, passed below us. The rear-window glass shattered and simultaneously the windshield exploded. The car rolled to a complete stop, and the driver stumbled out, blood spreading across his chest. Two men taking refuge in a doorway rushed to the man's aid and dragged him out of sight. The car began smoking and another pair of men darted out from

From one of our patients came this photo of the corpse of a palace guard.

shelter, pushed the car to the curb, and beat the fire with their jackets.

Tweedie and Flo, along with other hospital personnel, appeared on the balcony. A head was located across the hall. We decided to take a look from a different vantage point, since by now the balcony was crowded. The three of us climbed atop the commode and peered out the window. Another volley of shots crackled, and cement sprayed in all directions. We ducked out of sight, realizing *we* were being fired on, and decided to return to our units.

During the remainder of my shift, I wondered about the lack of detailed information forthcoming from any quarter. None of us needed to have a picture painted. Clearly, a crisis was at hand. But none of us really knew where we stood.

It was not uncommon for the embassy to issue periodic bulletins advising American personnel not to leave their locations. Armed Forces Radio Service had broadcast such a bulletin earlier in the day. Regardless, all of us made every effort to arrive for our duty, since we were medical personnel performing critical tasks. Therefore, I was not too surprised when Jan arrived for her P.M. duty. She was understandably shaken.

All of us reported to her in the normal change of shift routine. When we had a few moments, I inquired about Elaine, who had the day off. An incredible story unfolded. Elaine had been browsing in the Central Market during the late morning. While perusing merchandise she became aware, abruptly, of gunfire. The throng of shoppers heard the sound as well. They seemed for a moment frozen in place, as if they were confirming in their minds that this gunfire was different. It was not the single shot or explosion they were accustomed to.

In the next instant, a stampede of incredible size began. Pushing and shouting in panic, shoppers rushed for the market exits. Driven along by the shoving crowd, Elaine found herself on the street. The gunfire increased. She wanted to return to the apartment pronto. Her attempts to hail a cab failed, and she headed down Le Loi Street. Suddenly someone grabbed her arm, dragging her unceremoniously into a shop. It was a dark and small place. The shopkeeper was earnest in his efforts to detain her. Elaine did not protest and remained in "friendly captivity" until a lull in the gunfire, some time later. Finally she bolted from the shop, running nearly all the way to the Brink. Jan told us that Elaine had arrived scared senseless, quaking in her boots.

At 1700, Flo, Tweedie, and I received permission to return to quarters. We got into the chauffeured staff car and traveled three miles through a nearly vacant city. Destruction was surprisingly minimal, from what we could see. The quiet was uneasy—anxious. I had the feeling that the respite could explode at any moment.

The Ham Nghi was located just five blocks from the presidential palace. Our Friday evening was spent waiting and listening. Occasionally, one of the Army officers in our building checked in on us, and other tales were shared. Some officers had been in their quarters when the strike on the palace occurred. They recounted the scene—an incredible aerial attack, the palace defense, an eruption of gunfire on Ham Nghi Street below—all of it observed from front-row seats instead of from our balcony seats.

At the Saigon River, fuel farms were blazing with great intensity. The glow of the fire tinted the immediate landscape an eerie orange. Gunfire crackled sporadically from pockets around the city. We maintained a self-imposed blackout. Most of Saigon was pitch black. The radio chattered about nothing in particular, just the normal programming. The hourly news updates spoke of world events everywhere except where it counted—Saigon. Instead of timely, accurate information on the coup, we listened to the Top 40. It was ominous and ludicrous. I felt that at any moment the blackness would rupture.

At 2000, I heard the characteristic clank of heavy steel treads moving across the paved street. The sound came from Le Loi Street, around the corner from us. A tank. It fired a round that grunted, then impacted in the distance. My God, I remember thinking, is there going to be a tank fight in the middle of downtown Saigon? Shells exploded all around us. At least one 105-mm howitzer was being fired from the edge of the city. The assault seemed to be centered on the presidential palace—and we were in the middle.

Great smoking holes were blown into the roofs of buildings nearby. The Ham Nghi was showered with flying tile, glass, and shrapnel. The shells came whistling in, the blast effect tremendous. We felt concussions that left no doubt that we were front and center and not too secure. Safety aside, the three of us viewed the events from the balcony. Red tracer ammunition crisscrossed the night sky. Suddenly, one of the rounds displayed a trajectory aimed directly at us. Heads down and then it was gone overhead. That was close enough for Tweedie and Flo.

The battle acoustics were unique in the confines of the city. The din seemed to be intensified and funneled upward by the paved streets and buildings. All the noise headed straight up to the seventh deck. The concussions rocked us. Phase two of the assault began, and by midnight we decided to find a safer spot within the building.

Along with the Army officers, we congregated in the fourth-deck stairwell next to the elevator shaft. If the building took a direct hit, we felt we were in the most secure spot. No one wanted to be much closer to the street, since we couldn't identify the troops taking up posts.

All of us were eager to know something of the situation, to have some estimate of the coup in progress. For the first time, I remembered my short-wave radio and dashed upstairs. I heard a whine and then a deafening explosion as a shell hit a rooftop directly across the street. A wave of roof tile crashed against our building front. I was out of the apartment in record time.

The seven of us gathered around the radio and listened to a BBC broadcast from London relayed through Sidney to Saigon. Finally there was news—the announcer spoke of a coup attempt currently in progress in Saigon. He further mentioned that heavy fighting was ongoing in the streets, yet no one was certain who was fighting whom. Ironically, we who were sitting in the midst of the fighting were no better informed than the BBC announcer.

Our group began a discussion of the situation. We wondered whether the coup attempt would be successful. There was no doubt that American military personnel would feel the effects of a failed coup attempt. The politics and military strategies were complex. Diem, the duly appointed leader, stood to be replaced by a military junta. Anything might happen.

In the quick return to my room, I had grabbed my notepad. There was a light in the stairwell. I jotted down my impressions as shells exploded in the streets and gunfire crackled in the distance. It was a letter to my parents. As I wrote, I wondered if it would ever be received.

At 0330 on Saturday morning, 2 November, an all-out attack on the presidential palace began. The moon had risen. It was huge, orange, and gorgeous—a "tropical" moon. World War II flyers called such a moon a bomber's moon. We could call it a gunner's moon, since the city's buildings were perfectly silhouetted for the artillerymen. Throughout a sleepless night, I had watched the activity in the streets. Where a single tank had parked earlier, I now counted twenty-seven tanks and armored personnel carriers. There were two hundred troops marching slowly behind the vehicles—a ghostly procession illuminated by the strangely ethereal moonlight. And whose troops were they?

We had packed bags in the event we had to leave in a hurry. As I looked down on the scene, I speculated that we just might be needing them. The troops, fully armed, assumed posts in doorways. They were shadows, waiting. But for what? I couldn't tell. The artillery shelling resumed, and the troops moved toward the palace. It was, I assumed, the final assault.

The four of us waited. Gunfire was so intense we couldn't safely observe the action from the balcony. At one point, a brilliant white light bathed our room. It was blinding. Magnesium flares suspended from parachutes drifted over the Ham Nghi. I hoped they were strays. But there was no doubt that we were exposed to the gunner—we were vulnerable. Tweedie and Flo were agitated; I was annoyed. The intense flare light would outline the Ham Nghi as a target. Instead of heading for the stairwell, we sat tight, holding our collective breath as the parachutes drifted downward and darkness returned.

The coup had been in progress for fourteen hours. I wondered what was happening at Duong Duong. Our phone was working, but we received no calls from the hospital. Tweedie in particular would be needed if the situation was serious. I took the phone's silence as a sign that American casualties were minimal.

In the final moments of the attack, just before dawn, the firing intensified to a devastating volume. Our faces were blackened with soot; acrid cordite fumes from the explosions of gunpowder burned our eyes. The concussions from hours of exploding shells left us with pounding headaches. Then, at 0630, the assault stopped. A white flag fluttered in the distance. I could tell that it had been raised over the palace compound. The coup was over.

With the arrival of daylight, we were able to view the results of the shelling, at least around the Market area. The roofs of the surrounding buildings had holes five feet in diameter. Rubble, roof tiles, and broken glass lay everywhere. Looking at the devastation around us, I found it remarkable and downright lucky that we had been spared a direct hit.

With the cessation of fighting, Radio Saigon announced that the Diem government had been overthrown. Like ants pouring from an anthill, celebrants filled the streets. The crowds were jubilant. Young people waving flags jumped onto tanks and rode triumphantly through the city. Some sought out businesses known to be linked to the deposed government and looted and burned them.

Among the first to be destroyed was the office of *The Times of Vietnam*, which was an English-language progovernment paper. Five buildings away a crowd stormed another newspaper office. Presses, equipment, furniture, and giant rolls of paper were heaped on the pavement. A group of men overturned the paper's Volkswagen bus on top of the heap and set it ablaze. It burned for hours.

In close proximity to us, a theater was torched and a police station was grenaded and burned. We were surrounded by uncontrollable fires, and this posed a serious problem. The fire trucks were of the ancient, pumper variety. They filled up at the Saigon River and tried to return to the buildings. This was nearly impossible to accomplish, because the crowds refused to permit the trucks to pass. It seemed hopeless anyway—rather like flicking a thimbleful of water into an ocean.

Among the results of the coup was that it lifted the oppression of living in a police state. Some evidence was observable from our balcony. Below us and next door was a Vietnamese nightclub. The previous government had not permitted dancing. Suddenly, music to accompany a then-popular dance, the twist, blared. While Chubby Checker sang, the Vietnamese danced. How they had learned the twist was a mystery to me. There was, however, no doubt that they were enjoying it.

At first light, I began shooting pictures. We remained on our rooftop all day watching the circus below. During the afternoon, an L-19 and a DC-3 appeared overhead. Down came a shower of pink, green, and yellow paper. The papers were leaflets that informed the populace of the overthrow and announced that the Military Revolutionary Council was now in control.

On Sunday morning, Tweedie and I ventured out. We saw first the destruction immediately around the Ham Nghi. Corners had been blown off buildings. Walls were pock-marked, riddled by automatic-weapon fire. Some buildings displayed huge holes in their walls. The heavier shells had sheared off lampposts and trees. Debris littered the streets.

Water mains had ruptured. Telephone lines were down in some areas. Hundreds of windows were shattered. We approached a black Volkswagen beetle that was so riddled by gunfire, it looked like a piece of black lace.

We arrived at the palace compound, a smoking ruin. We entered through a gaping hole in the perimeter concrete wall. Broken tank treads lay scattered on the lawn. Defending soldiers had been blown out of their shoes, which lay everywhere. Pools of blood had congealed into dark puddles. The stench of cordite and burning rubber and debris hung heavy. Trapped within the confines of the walls, the stench intensified in the heat. Charred hulks of vehicles, one containing a body, stood randomly in the yard. I photographed everything.

Later, one of the Army officers quartered in our building, himself a member of the infantry, told us that many men wearing the Combat Infantryman's Badge had been subjected to less gunfire than we had during the seventeen hours of the coup. He acknowledged our calmness and coolness under fire. This, I knew, was as it should be. We were, after all, military nurses.

NINE

The Fragility of the Status Quo

THE SUDDEN DRAMA of the November coup d'état had momentarily served as a relief valve to reduce the pressure-cooker atmosphere of Saigon. The action was a change from the "ordinary extraordinary"— the terrorist episodes, the communications problems, the fragile political climate, and the growing escalation of the war—which made this such a unique billet. Duong Duong had survived the coup. Aside from a few bullet holes in the walls and a little debris, the hospital was shipshape. Amazingly, we had received no patients with injuries directly related to the revolt. Instead, our medical ward was tending to routine cases and a few not-so-routine cases.

Ailments caused by consumption of local food and water were always with us; often, the health-care givers joined the patients. Disaster struck during my Saigon tour while I was temporary acting senior nurse. One hundred percent of the staff were suffering the effects of amebiasis. This is a miserable affliction—a parasitic infection acquired by ingestion of food or drink that has been contaminated by intestinal excreta containing amoebic cysts. It was widespread in Southeast Asia, where standards of sanitation and food handling were lacking. The lower intestinal wall is attacked, causing the formation of ulcers. The onset of symptoms was often sudden, with associated abdominal cramplike pain, diarrhea, nausea, and vomiting. Prostration could be severe enough to require morphine to ease abdominal pain. Worse, cysts could invade the liver, resulting in life-threatening liver abscesses. The pleura, right lung, and pericardium of the heart could also be attacked.

At the time of this outbreak, we were short-staffed and could not afford to lose one more nurse or corpsman to the sick list. It was reserved for only the most acute cases. I hadn't completely recovered from my first episode of amebiasis when I contracted it again. I was so worried about liver complications that I never missed taking a pill during the two twenty-day treatment periods.

A number of patients were admitted for treatment of tropical diseases. While these patients would typically bypass my Intensive Care and Recovery units, I did have responsibility for their care on the P.M. shift.

Those of us practicing professions within the medical field in the northern temperate climates rarely see diseases indigenous to the tropical zones. We read about them in our student textbooks, discuss them briefly in our classrooms, and seldom think of them again. Frequently, I used to come across the most vivid descriptions of these diseases in history books and novels. Once I had arrived in Vietnam, I found myself with the opportunity to observe and treat these cases for the first time.

Dengue fever, or breakbone fever, is one illness found in southern latitudes. It is an acute febrile disease characterized by a sudden onset of headache, fever, and prostration, discomfort in the joints and muscles, and a painful rash that appears simultaneously, with a second rise in temperature following an afebrile state. Although none of us had dealt with dengue fever before, we had no trouble recognizing the symptoms. The causative agent is a filtrable virus that is mosquito-borne. There is no vaccination against it.

Routine supply flights from the Delta often brought soldiers who were afflicted with the disease. A typical case found the patient hospital-bound for a minimum of two weeks. There is no specific treatment for the virus, and the best that we could do was to treat the symptoms. Dengue is rarely fatal, and in my experience even the most severe cases eventually recovered following careful monitoring and supportive nursing care.

All American personnel received immunizations before arriving in country. In the case of malaria, however, prevention was effected by taking a daily dose of medication. Sometimes this medication routine was overlooked by the troops. During my Saigon assignment, malaria was the number-one cause of days lost by the United States troops stationed there. It put more men out of action than did combat injuries. Many soldiers injured in battle returned to duty in a few days; malaria kept them on the sick list for an average of thirty-five days.

Malaria may be described as an acute or chronic and often recurrent febrile parasitic disease, characterized by periodic attacks of chills followed by high fever, the presence of parasites within the red blood cells, frequent enlargement of the spleen, and sometimes jaundice. The infection develops following the bite of an infected mosquito or by the transfusion of infected blood.

Each of the malarial types presents a different biological picture, making a differential diagnosis necessary. Black water fever, which is caused by one of the four types of malarial parasites, held the most interest for me.

Late one November afternoon, we admitted a young Army captain who appeared to be acutely ill. His condition worsened so rapidly that he was moved that evening from the medical ward to my ICU. By employing blood-smear laboratory studies, our internist diagnosed the soldier's malaria as *Plasmodium falciparum*.

The patient was suffering from chills, fever in the 104- to 106-degree range, and a severe headache. Later we observed increased drowsiness, delirium, and mental confusion. It was our first case of malaria, and I broke out a tropical disease textbook for the purpose of reviewing the symptoms. I wanted my corpsmen to be fully briefed on the interpretation of these signs and symptoms, since we had by now a dangerously ill patient. We fully realized how ill he was when he began going into delirium and confusion. To us this indicated impending cerebral malaria, which has a high fatality rate.

We worked for hours in an attempt to lower his very high body temperature. Meanwhile, we administered large doses of one of the antimalarial drugs specifically used in *Plasmodium falciparum* malaria. He hardly responded. His urinary output was watched closely for signs of the black water form of malaria. This dreaded complication resulted when hemolysis, or breakup of the red cells, occurred. The cells were then excreted through the kidneys, giving the urine a very dark appearance—hence the name black water fever. In addition, our patient began to display symptoms of shock, anemia, and jaundice—all results of hemolysis.

We continued with the prescribed treatment. After hours of alcohol-sponging, ice packs, and fans playing over his body, his temperature began to fall; shock subsided, and he began to respond. We worked so terribly hard to save this young soldier's life that when the doctor told us he thought the patient would live, we felt a great sense of relief and very rewarded. It is a wonderful thing to realize that one has been instrumental in the saving of a life, particularly the life of a young person in his prime. Adding to the satisfaction was the fact that we had seen and saved our first black water fever case. The captain made a complete recovery and returned to full duty.

By the middle of November, I had written six letters to my parents and received six back. Their letters (written by Mom) were newsy and upbeat. Snoopy was thriving, the family was well, Dad and Mom were both working hard. Thanksgiving was drawing close. I found myself reminiscing. I knew there was snow at home in northwestern Pennsylvania—sometimes deep snow, transforming our property into a scene resembling a Norman Rockwell painting. Our woods were broad, sweeping vistas of hickory, oak, maple, and pine trees—so unlike the palms and jungle foliage of Vietnam.

I found myself missing little things like the deer standing at the edge of the tree line, eyeing the salt lick we kept on the flagstone patio. We'd watch as they cautiously approached, sometimes several at a time, enjoying the salt lick and then wandering off toward a nearby stream. Pleasant memories of a world 12,000 miles away.

During the postcoup days in Saigon, the routine at Duong Duong continued status quo. That condition changed abruptly on 22 November 1963. At 0530, the embassy telephoned the hospital to inform the officer of the day that President John F. Kennedy had been assassinated. The oncoming morning staff was in turn informed by the night crew. I was not among that day's crew, so I did not hear of the tragedy until 0900.

It was my day off—Saturday, 23 November in Vietnam—a day that began unremarkably. Sitting down to breakfast, I turned on my shortwave radio and tuned in to the daily program broadcast by the Voice of America. Because the program was relayed through the Philippines to the Armed Forces Radio Service in Saigon, the signal was rather poor and fluctuated. Despite the inconsistent quality of the broadcast, I nevertheless realized that I was listening to the details of an assassination. But who had been assassinated?

The broadcaster sounded oddly tense and excited. I was literally hanging onto every word. "Kennedy . . . " The signal faded. I listened intently. Again the president's name was spoken, and I was stunned. I realized then that it was the president of the United States who had been shot.

As I sat there, attempting to organize my thoughts, the phone rang. Tweedie was calling me to tell me the news. Details at the time were fragmented. She offered little in addition to what I had heard. Thi Cong and Thi Ba, attending to the chores, were oblivious to the news. I lingered at the table, lost in my own thoughts, wondering what on earth had happened in Dallas.

An hour later, Tweedie and Flo arrived home for lunch. Together we listened to the broadcast, slowly assimilating the details until a clearer picture began to emerge. We wondered what would happen in Vietnam, what impact—if any—Kennedy's death would have. Would the war effort escalate rapidly or, at the other extreme, would it de-escalate? There were no answers.

Besides the American community in Vietnam, others were shocked. There were Vietnamese who liked and supported President Kennedy. Just days earlier, a plaque honoring Kennedy had been placed in front of the Catholic basilica in Saigon. Ambassador Lodge and General Khanh had been at the dedication.

We continued to receive bits and pieces of information over the next several days. There was no television coverage. There were very few photographs. When Lee Harvey Oswald was shot, we were again in a state of confusion. It was another several days before we learned how an alleged assassin was assassinated. The double slaying had a terrific

Ambassador Henry Cabot Lodge at the dedication of a plaque honoring President John F. Kennedy, days before Kennedy's assassination

impact on those of us half a world away. I wondered what the impact must have been for Americans at home.

The twenty-fourth of November began bright and sunny. At noon, Thi Cong summoned us to the balcony. Flo, Tweedie, and I looked down upon a remarkable sight. Thousands of Vietnamese students, five abreast and carrying English-language placards, formed a procession that moved along Ham Nghi Street toward the Central Market. Banners eulogized Kennedy in what was the first pro-American demonstration we had witnessed since arriving in Vietnam. At the height of the march, the sky opened and a deluge poured down. The marchers continued. It was a poignant, unforgettable sight.

By the end of November, morale among those of us stationed in Saigon had sunk considerably. Thanksgiving Day, 27 November, passed. The annual Army-Navy football game would have been played on the following Saturday, 30 November. Because of President Kennedy's death, the game was postponed until 7 December, with kickoff scheduled for 0100 hours, Saigon time. It was played at the urging of the Kennedy family, to whom the game was dedicated.

AFRS's fluctuating broadcast signal was a source of irritation as we listened to the game. Just when a big play occurred, the signal would fade, leaving us in the dark. In the end Navy won, 21–15. It was Roger Staubach's Heisman Trophy Year, as Navy enjoyed a 9–1 season. That one game lifted our spirits at a time when it seemed almost nothing would.

The coup d'état had given us some reason for optimism. American military personnel had thought that with the new regime, the war effort in general would become better focused. We had hoped that an increase in solidarity within the South Vietnamese government would lead to a revival in the war effort and a successful conclusion. The reverse, however, was the case.

I pulled no punches, and my correspondence home reflected my mood. I was depressed. The war effort was deteriorating from bad to worse, in my view. Kennedy's death had only worsened an already bad situation.

Worse yet, our armed forces lost several helicopters and planes to VC ground fire. We did not attend to the casualties from these episodes, because everyone was killed. Nothing was going our way. Then, late in the month, a Special Forces camp located near the outskirts of Saigon was the scene of a VC attack. Several "trusted" workers there were in reality Viet Cong. One night, they started an attack within the camp. Four American soldiers were captured, and many ARVN troops were wounded or killed. Weapons, ammunition, and several thousand dollars were stolen.

The four captured Americans were later paraded naked through villages and hamlets. A fifth American was asleep in his tent when one of the guerrillas tossed a grenade through the flap. Although severely wounded from the grenade, he managed to shoot and kill the VC and escape, crawling through the muddy rice paddies with the VC in pursuit. Somehow, he eluded his would-be captors and reached safety, where he was found and brought to Duong Duong.

The grenade had left him with multiple shrapnel wounds. We cleaned, debrided, removed the shrapnel, and sutured the wounds. After the surgery, I settled him into his bed in the ICU. He regained consciousness and was beginning to recover.

One day, he developed a severe psychotic episode, exhibiting homicidal tendencies. At six feet four inches, and weighing over two hundred pounds, he had been trained to kill with one blow. He leapt from his bed and became aggressive. It took several corpsmen a considerable time to restrain him. At one point, he became so violent that he literally tossed the corpsmen around the room, bouncing them off the walls. I ran for the leather wrist and ankle restraints. It took five of us to fasten them. A doctor arrived and injected him with a sedative. Since he was potentially dangerous and because we were not equipped for psychiatric treatment, he was medevaced to the Philippines.

During my tour of duty in Vietnam, we received few psychiatric casualties. One study I read at the time estimated twelve such cases per thousand a year—a remarkably low figure. The study further speculated that the low figure might be explained by the fact that the tour of duty for soldiers serving in Vietnam was one year. There were no long-term battles fought in the front lines along conventional warfare techniques, which would have subjected the men to prolonged and heavy artillery fire. They were also dedicated, professional career soldiers. They were, for the most part, in Vietnam on a voluntary basis. All that would later change.

It was becoming a pleasure to care for these career soldiers. It seemed that a speedy recovery was their number-one priority. They wanted to return to duty as quickly as possible. Denis Warner, in his very knowledgeable book *The Last Confucian*, describes [American soldiers] as "superb, an elite of unprecedented quality and dedication.

They knew their jobs as soldiers and they were equally effective in their relations with the Civil Guard, the Self Defense Corps and the people themselves."*

There were, of course, some bright spots. Duong Duong was doing its job, providing excellent care. I was expanding my professional knowledge, treating diseases that I might never again encounter. Most important, our patients, American military personnel, were some of the finest young men in the Armed Services—the cream of the crop.

*Denis Warner, *The Last Confucian* (Baltimore: Penguin Books, 1964), 35.

TEN

Christmas, and a
Wish Fulfilled

AS THE HOLIDAY SEASON approached, there was little time to remi-
nisce. Of our original group of nurses, one had returned prematurely
to the States: Jan Barcott had contracted a particularly severe case of
dengue fever and had been medevaced out of Saigon. In her absence, the
rest of us assumed her duties until a replacement arrived. We would be
busy, and I liked it that way. We were literally riding a roller coaster. At
any moment, almost anything could happen. Low morale tugged at all
of us. But all of us knew that it could be worse.

It would be a different kind of Christmas season for most of us. No
snow, no fresh-cut trees to decorate. I would miss these things and
many more. But, as always, life is what you make it.

Someone had sent an artificial tree for our quarters. Penny had
drawn on her considerable craft skills to construct ornaments and decorations. And packages from home arrived. My own contained fudge, a
pair of pj's, a bottle of my favorite 4711 cologne, soaps, and a color portrait of Snoopy, along with the black-and-white proofs. My spirits were
temporarily lifted.

Following dinner on Christmas Eve, Tweedie and I were in the process of sorting and wrapping presents to distribute to our friends when
we were called to the Emergency Room for an unusual case. At the
hospital, we found Walt Johnson already intent on examining a young
man, specifically his throat in the area of the cricoid cartilage, or Adam's
apple.

The patient seemed to be in respiratory distress and was obviously
shaken. Walt briefed us on the details of the injury. The patient, an
Army man, and one of our staff corpsmen had been in a fight. As the

argument escalated, the corpsman shot the soldier. The gun was fired at close range, but miraculously the bullet struck the cricoid cartilage at an angle, causing it to deflect without even penetrating the skin. There was a small ecchymotic (bruised) area appearing directly at the point of impact, as well as a slight degree of edema (swelling). Since there was the possibility of a pending tracheotomy, Tweedie and I had been summoned.

The soldier's distraught emotional state caused a manifestation known as hyperventilation, in which too much carbon dioxide is lost through rapid breathing. This in turn precipitates an imbalance in the normal acid-alkaline body chemistry and, among other symptoms, gives the patient the impression that he is choking or unable to get his breath.

The simple treatment of calming a patient slows his too-rapid breathing and allows the carbon dioxide to rebuild, allaying his symptoms. While Tweedie prepared a tracheotomy tray, I held the young man's hand and tried to reassure him. Walt and I succeeded in calming the man, and soon his breathing returned to normal. He was detained in the hospital overnight only for observation of possible increased edema in the throat, which would cause an airway obstruction. Fortunately, the swelling did not increase; he was discharged on Christmas Day. We were all convinced that this soldier's guardian angel had been on duty that night.

It was indeed a unique Christmas. We did not have the chance to attend the midnight service, arriving back to quarters quite late. Christmas Day dawned hot and steamy. From our balcony we observed the streets below, the marketplace, and the vendors. It was business as usual in Saigon.

In *The Observer*, a weekly newspaper published by the Army for service personnel, we read a letter to Santa:

Dear Santa:

We wonder if you could tow along a little of your North Pole climate, and maybe cut it loose over Saigon. This request shows how unselfish we are, as a lot of other folks would benefit. But easy on the snow, huh? You know what an inch of snow will do to Saigon traffic. We'd have the world's biggest auto junkyard in five minutes . . . Come on now, Santa: they just look like junk now, but they all still run. Aw, there's a whole bunch of stuff we'd like, Santa, but you're gonna need the space for the troops in the field. Now don't go getting a runner shot off your sleigh by ground fire out there, and be sure and make your reindeer wear their flak suits. You know how it is: cruise at altitude and make steep approaches into those outposts. And we know how your red suit's traditional, and all that, but it might be the better part of valor to pick up a nice set of camouflaged jungle *fatigues for "safety." Tell you what to bring the troops out there. Most of all, probably, if you could pick up any stray mail from home, they'd like that. They'd also like some fresh milk, probably as much as they'd appreciate any new type bug spray, and if you have any kind of hot-lead repellent, by all means bring them some of that. We know that what we are asking is a long order, and the odds are against filling most of it, but we'd thought we'd give it a tumble anyway . . . ** *

We had invited the Brink girls over for brunch and an exchange of gifts. A green sheet from the OR served as a tablecloth. As usual, we improvised. The get-together provided a nice respite from the previous night's emergency.

I was not scheduled for duty on Christmas Day. The girls who were left for their P.M. shift. A couple of us made the most of the tropical sun and the 95-degree temperatures by sunbathing.

For me, the holiday season provided time for continued reflection. I had been in Vietnam for three and a half months. I felt that in that short time, I had seen and participated in more compelling events than most people are exposed to in a lifetime. Still, my tour of duty was only one-quarter complete. What would the next nine months hold?

The coming year, 1964, was the Year of the Dragon, according to the traditional Oriental lunar calendar. The belief was that every sixty years, big events such as wars and natural disasters were likely to repeat themselves. An ancient Vietnamese proverb said, "In the Year of the Dragon everybody keeps his food for himself."

In the previous cycle, the Year of the Dragon (1904) was particularly disastrous because a violent typhoon hit the central coastal area. Famine due to the crop destruction and death by drowning were widespread.

The 1964 Year of the Dragon and the escalating conflict known as the Vietnam War ultimately fulfilled the ancient proverb's prophecies of repeated cycles to an even greater extent than the events of 1904 had. Typhoons Iris and Jean catastrophically devastated the Central Highlands. Torrential rains and flooding left seven thousand Vietnamese dead and a million homeless. Typhoon Kate threatened to add even more devastation, but she deviated from her course at the last moment, sparing Vietnam. Iris and Jean became known as the worst natural disasters suffered by Vietnam in modern history. It was indeed a time when prudent individuals looked out for themselves and kept the fruits of their labors close at hand.

*Staff Sergeant Bob Reed, USAF, "A Pocketful of Notes," *The Observer,* December 1963.

Morale remained at a low ebb for many of us. But I looked forward to the coming New Year, ancient prophecies notwithstanding. In January, I would leave for a brief visit to Angkor Wat and Angkor Thom.

For a very long time, it had been my desire to visit the ancient Khmer ruins of Angkor Wat and Angkor Thom, far up in the northern Cambodian jungle. Since Cambodia and Vietnam were adjoining countries, relatively little flying time was consumed when making the trip; thus the excursion could be made on a weekend, although a week would have been ideal.

Prince Norodom Sihanouk, the Cambodian head of state, was becoming increasingly intransigent. He had recently announced to the world that he would no longer accept American assistance, and that all Americans attached to the various assistance organizations in Cambodia would have to leave, with the exception of the American embassy staff.

If we were ever going to go to Cambodia, it had to be soon. Penny, Tweedie, and I planned to make the trip on the weekend of 11 and 12 January 1964. The week prior was consumed in cutting red tape—and there seemed to be no end to it. We had a saying—"Nothing is ever easy in Vietnam"—which was surely borne out by this excursion.

Since Vietnam and Cambodia had severed relations, the French embassy was handling the affairs of both countries. It was necessary to obtain a Cambodian visa, which we were able to do with little difficulty. However, we had other problems up to the very last minute, and we nearly missed the plane.

When we checked through Vietnamese customs at Tan Son Nhut, the inspector insisted that our passports were not in order. We couldn't understand, because of his poor English, what was missing. After a long harangue, he placed a phone call, indicating that whatever we didn't have could be obtained from an office in downtown Saigon. Irritated, we took a taxi back into the city and found the office and the proper official, only to be told we didn't need a Vietnamese exit or entrance visa since we were American military. Only then did we realize that the customs inspector had arbitrarily requested these visas. Even after we presented our military travel orders, ID cards, immunization records, and passports, he still seemed to fail to realize that we were American military. When things of this nature happened, we never really knew if it was a deliberate form of harassment or an honest mistake. In time, we began to feel that it was a case of the former.

After the meaningless, hot, ten-mile round-trip back into Saigon, we were sure that we had missed the plane. To our surprise, we had not. We again passed through customs and encountered the same inspector. There was no mistaking his smug look.

The plane was late in departing because Pochentong Airport in Cambodia had been closed for a two-hour period. The reason for this was that President Sukarno of Indonesia was flying to Cambodia, so while his plane was arriving and official ceremonies were being conducted, all air traffic was halted. It was lucky for us.

The flight from Saigon to Phnom Penh, the capital city of Cambodia, was made via an ancient Royal Air Cambodge DC-4. Many of the Oriental airliners were very uncomfortable for Westerners. Since Asiatics are small of stature, seats with decreased leg room had been installed. This had enlarged the seating capacity probably by half again as much as the original seating configuration. Penny, the tiniest of our group, fit nicely into the airliner seats and flew comfortably. Tweedie, at five feet two inches, fit nicely and voiced no complaints. But when I, at five feet five inches and with long legs, folded into the seat, my knees practically touched my chest. I could have avoided such discomfort, but I wanted that window seat.

I was happy to finally land, deplane, and take a much-needed walk. As always, the plane was as hot as a blast furnace, so the air-conditioned terminal at our stopover point in Phnom Penh was a real oasis.

The connecting flight north to Siem Reap was made in an even more decrepit DC-3 that was jammed to capacity. We took seats in the aft section of the craft. Thinking I heard the cackling of chickens, I turned and saw a crate of them in the tail section. A woman passenger took a disparaging view of the trip when she discovered that her bright red coat was covered with chicken droppings. She was understandably irate, chewing out all the airline personnel—to no avail.

Our course took us over what seemed like endless reaches of wild, apparently uninhabited thick green jungle. Other times the aircraft paralleled the Tonle Sap River as it wended its way south to Phnom Penh. Then, in the distance, we saw the curving shoreline of the huge Tonle Sap Lake. It was so large that we seemed to fly forever over it.

Normally, Tonle Sap Lake covers an area of nearly nineteen hundred square miles. During the latter portion of the rainy season—July to October—the river flows in reverse, causing the lake's level to rise some forty feet above normal. The lake increases in size nearly three and a half times. The Cambodians claimed that Tonle Sap had a higher fish content than any other lake in the world—about sixteen tons of fish per square mile. As we flew along its shores we could look down upon the fishing boats, their sails white dots on the deep blue water, and the picturesque floating villages built by the fishermen.

The sun was beginning to dip below the giant gum trees encircling the ancient ruins as we approached the airport at Siem Reap. Against the waning sunlight, the Angkor Wat and Angkor Thom ruins were immensely impressive as they rose from the jungle floor. Our approach took us directly over the magnificent temple remnants at low altitude.

It was still daylight when we arrived at the Grand Hotel, located on the outskirts of town. After registering, we changed our money to Cambodian riels and purchased tickets for the evening's entertainment.

Every Saturday night, the Royal Cambodian Ballet Company entertained the hotel guests, offering dance that has remained unchanged in style since its origins centuries ago. The performance is given on an ancient stage of one of the main temples of Angkor Wat, and the audience sits atop one of the crumbling walls.

The performance was spectacular. The costumes were gorgeous, made from heavy, rich brocades and fine silks, all in brilliant colors with threads of silver and gold woven throughout each costume. The traditional headdress was typically Cambodian—silver and gold, in the design of the lotus bud and the naga serpent, ancient sacred symbols.

Sitting in the midst of the lovely ancient ruins deep in the jungle evoked a sense of well-being that I had not experienced since my arrival in Southeast Asia. The jasmine night was balmy and the bright stars hanging low against a velvet blue-black tropical sky were visible through the tops of the huge old trees. There was no moon at all. We could hear night birds calling, and occasionally an elephant trumpeting or a jungle cat screeching. The great towers, in the shape of lotus buds and serpents, were sharply outlined in silhouette against the night sky.

At the end of the performance, we reluctantly left our seats and, by candlelight, were escorted by small native boys along the paths through the ruins to the waiting buses. How wonderful it had been to relax in the open, away from the rigors of war.

We arose early Sunday morning, anxious to explore. As we moved through the hotel lobby, we picked our way through props for the movie *Lord Jim,* which was being filmed on location in the ruins.

Angkor Wat was the ancient city of the Khmers, a civilization that flourished from the ninth to the fifteenth centuries. In time the Khmers were either killed or put to flight by the Thais; the last of the survivors had fled by 1432.

The civilization became a lost one, as it faded from memory for four hundred years. Its ruins were not discovered until the 1860s—and then only by accident. There were stories and legends that such a civilization had existed, but nothing factual was known. With the accidental discovery, legend became fact.

In those climes of tropical rain forests, the jungle becomes thick and engulfing in a short time. Gum trees, which grow to the monstrous height of two hundred feet, caused the greatest damage to the structures as their roots split and cracked the ancient walls and floors. Restoration was being done with the help of l'Ecole Française d'Extrème Orient, a French restoration society. Financed primarily by private contributions, with some government funding, the work was proceeding slowly. At times, when funds were particularly low, the work came to a virtual halt. At the time of my Vietnam tour, the Cambodian government had allotted some funds for the project.

For three hours, we climbed through the ruins and wandered up and down the dense, shadowy jungle trails. Elephants, tigers, panthers, and cobras inhabited the temples at night. With the arrival of morning and visitors, they drifted off into the seclusion of the deeper jungle. Heat and humidity became intense, and several of the older people in the party suffered severely. The ruins (as well as the previous evening's performance) were a photographer's dream.

Unfortunately, we simply did not have enough time for side trips on elephant back or in a Land Rover, to more obscure ruins. How disgruntled I was. I had the opportunity of fulfilling a lifetime ambition and was only able to spend a few hours among the ruins.

Early afternoon was taken up preparing for our 1500 flight back to Phnom Penh. In clearing the hotel, we became involved in a distressing argument concerning our papers. We were unable to convince the hotel authorities that we needed no Vietnamese exit or entry visas. It seemed to us that their chief concern was that Vietnam would not permit us to reenter, and they certainly did not want to be stuck with us.

After a half-hour discussion, during which we held our tempers in check and tried to overcome the ever-present language barrier, they finally concluded that the only thing for us to do was sign a waiver absolving them of any responsibility should the Vietnamese authorities not permit us to reenter. We were careful in our perusal of the waiver. Still, it was with some trepidation that we eventually signed the document.

We had knowledge beforehand of a common occurrence that complicated a visitor's trip. When we changed our U.S. currency into Cambodian riels, we were careful to change a minimal amount. We knew that our riels would not be converted back to dollars; neither would we be permitted to take riels out of Cambodia. The unsuspecting tourist either forked over his remaining riels or was not permitted to leave the country.

One of the men in our group had exchanged his currency for riels in Hong Kong. He had obtained five thousand riels, roughly a hundred and fifty dollars. In compliance with the Cambodian customs declaration, he had honestly declared his Cambodian money upon entry. The entire sum was promptly confiscated. He was informed that it was illegal to bring Cambodian currency obtained elsewhere into the country—even though a perfectly legal exchange had been made in Hong Kong.

In protesting the "theft," he became so vociferous that he was threatened with jail if he did not cease and desist. Fortunately, he ceased and desisted, much poorer and much wiser concerning money matters Cambodian-style.

By now we had established a pattern. We were about to land in Phnom Penh, so we knew it was time for more harassment with the official over that old vexation, the Vietnamese visa. A police guard kept us under constant surveillance. When we adjourned to the ladies' room, a female officer picked up our trail, nearly entering my stall. I drew the line there, slamming the door in her face and quickly sliding the bolt. "*Choi oi*" was an appropriate sentiment. The Vietnamese expression held several meanings ranging from disgust to surprise. I found myself using the term often.

When our flight was called, we were happy to board the aircraft and escape the visa nonsense. Soon after crossing the Cambodian–South Vietnamese border, we looked down upon a firefight in progress in and around a burning village. It was unknown to us whether this was a Viet Cong stronghold under attack or a hamlet being attacked by the Viet Cong.

We landed at Tan Son Nhut and felt right at home, hearing the sound of 105s being fired somewhere in the vicinity. Nothing had changed in Saigon.

ELEVEN
Distinguished Visitors

JANUARY ALSO BROUGHT the first of several distinguished visitors to Duong Duong. The first was a Hollywood celebrity, to be followed by the commander of a U.S. Navy ship of the line and a five-year-old girl complete with entourage.

One evening, the patients and staff were treated to a pleasant surprise. Actor Raymond Burr arrived at the hospital unannounced, with no fanfare, no throng of publicity men. He walked in, and I recognized him instantly. "You're Perry Mason," I said. He smiled a big, warm grin and replied that he was. He explained that he was there to visit with the patients—if it could be arranged.

I was more than happy to arrange this. The evening was quiet; there were no incoming emergencies. Raymond Burr was an enormous man, well over six feet tall and burly, but soft-spoken and gentle. I accompanied him on his tour, introducing him to our patients. He spent a brief time with each of them, even taking phone numbers from Californians, promising to place a call to their families when he returned. Some asked for autographs, others were just happy to chat for a few moments. At each stop, Mr. Burr thanked our soldiers for what they were doing, always commending their efforts and wishing them good luck. It was easy to feel his overwhelming sincerity.

Mr. Burr spent a lot of time with the field units, too. He was not particularly interested in staying in Saigon—he wanted to be where the action was, to visit the Green Berets and the other troops. I learned that he even visited remote locations and isolated areas, often riding in the choppers. He ate with the troops and lived with them.

Some time after he visited Duong Duong, I heard an anecdote from someone who had spent time with him. It seemed that Mr. Burr had asked if there might be a spare set of fatigues that he could borrow. Having been in the field for awhile, he had run out of clean clothes. The men were happy to comply, but after an exhaustive search, not one set of fatigues large enough could be found. In fact, it seemed that there was not a large enough set to be found in the entire country. Finally a flight suit was located, and so Mr. Burr had a set of clean clothes to wear.

When he finished his hospital tour, he told me that he would try to return soon. He was that committed to the troops. True to his word, he did. One June night I was making rounds and walked into the lobby, to collide with Raymond Burr. He gave me a big bear hug, remembering me from his first visit. I asked him if he had made the phone calls promised earlier. He had, of course. Again he visited each bedside, boosting spirits along the way. His visit was the hot topic of conversation until lights out.

By January, a strategy to bring American warships fifty miles up the Saigon River from the South China Sea was implemented. Consequently, the Navy community as well as other Americans serving in Vietnam and the citizens of Saigon were treated to a visit from the USS *Providence*.

We all took great pride in this visit. The *Providence*, a guided-missile cruiser, was the flagship of the United States Seventh Fleet, commanded by Vice Adm. Thomas Moorer. When she arrived on 18 January, several of us went down to the Vietnamese Navy piers to welcome her.

I noted the precautions taken to safeguard the ship. Divers were alerted to look for deadly mines. Guns were trained from the deck of the ship toward the oppposite riverbank. Security was indeed heightened. And yet when we stepped aboard, it was like setting foot on home soil. The ship was sparkling clean—so American. We were taken on a tour with special emphasis placed on the hospital spaces. Afterward, we were invited to the wardroom for coffee and fresh-baked cookies. What a treat.

Later in the week, a hospital corpsman stationed on the ship stopped by Duong Duong to say hello. He also wanted to *cumshaw* some cholera vaccine to re-immunize the ship's company. The booster immunization was necessary because an epidemic was going full force in Saigon. I knew this corpsman from my Quantico days and agreed to hand over some vaccine if he would contribute adhesive tape to our dangerously low supply. He agreed to include two quarts of frozen milk in the deal.

A welcome visitor: the USS *Providence*

That evening, the ICU patients who were permitted to and the ward staff each enjoyed a glass. Fresh milk was a rarity, and we savored it to the last drop. But there was one more treat.

Before the ship left, Admiral Moorer and his staff visited the patients and hospital personnel. He was generous in his praise of our group, congratulating us on our care of the casualties and our other patients.

Tuyet Khanh was a cute, sweet five-year-old, the daughter of Gen. Nguyen Khanh, prime minister of South Vietnam. Tuyet was born with an extensive hemangioma: the right side of her face, including the white area of the eye, was covered with a deep purple birthmark that extended into the scalp.

The U.S. Embassy arranged for surgical removal of the hemangioma. A prominent plastic surgeon, Dr. Richard B. Stark, flew in from New York to perform the surgery. (U.S.-based civilian doctors came to Vietnam for one-month stays, performing operative procedures in their various specialties.) Tweedie administered the anesthesia, and I was assigned as OR circulating nurse.

General Khanh rose to power as a result of the bloodless coup d'état on 30 January. Viet Cong terrorist strikes increased following Khanh's takeover. Thus, safety was of great concern to General and Madame Khanh. When tiny Tuyet arrived, so did twelve ARVN soldiers.

Captain Fisichella greeted Tuyet, Madame Khanh, Tuyet's aunt, and her grandmother. In Vietnam, it is customary for family members to accompany a patient to the hospital and remain for the entire stay. This is because family members often provide the primary nursing care. Comdr. Ann Richman, recently arrived to fill the chief nurse vacancy created by the departure of Flo Alwyn for the States, and I welcomed the Khanhs and helped them settle into their rooms. They were given three small rooms off the hospital's rear entrance; this was our easily accessed "VIP Suite." The unreliable elevator was avoided completely.

Tuyet's preoperative workup filled the remainder of 4 March. Standard blood work, chest X-ray, history, and physical examination were required before surgery. The little girl was an excellent patient.

The staff attended to the medical aspects of Tuyet's stay under the watchful eyes of the ARVN soldiers. While I appreciated the need for additional security, the truth is, all sorts of problems arose. Ten Vietnamese hospital guards stood in place twenty-four hours a day. This became a logistical nightmare when a dozen more guards came aboard. They were stationed around the perimeter of the compound, in the guard towers, and on nearby roofs. On 5 March, two troops stood guard outside the Operating Room doors while Tuyet underwent surgery.

Duong Duong was filled to its hundred-bed capacity. The victims of the Kinh Do bombing were recovering, and we had many other patients. Tuyet's admission was not ideal timing, but it couldn't be helped. The plastic surgeon's availability dictated Tuyet's DOS (day of surgery). With twenty additional people suddenly underfoot, Charley's meal runs were taxed to the limit. He made frequent second trips to accommodate the Khanh entourage. The troops chattered incessantly, and our relatively quiet hospital environment disappeared. While we enjoyed Tuyet and her family, none of us needed the disruption.

The hospital atmosphere was charged on the morning of 5 March. Besides the presence of the head of state's family and the heightened security, we had other things to worry about; there are risks inherent with every surgical procedure and with every anesthetic.

Joe Craney, a bald, jovial corpsman, carried Tuyet down the steps to the Operating Room. Tweedie administered a general anesthetic. The surgery began on time and proceeded smoothly. I had not seen the re-

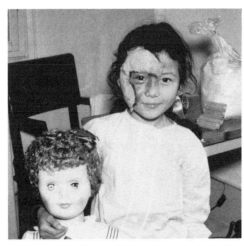

The captivating Tuyet, daughter of Gen. Nguyen Khanh, prime minister of South Vietnam

moval of a hemangioma, though I had participated in other plastic procedures. Dr. Stark was professional and a pleasure to assist. I was delighted that he was not a prima donna.

The procedure, which lasted approximately two hours, ended without incident. Afterward, the surgeon applied a large pressure dressing, exposing Tuyet's good eye. She remained in the OR to recover, and when she left in stable condition we all breathed a sigh of relief.

I made her comfortable and assumed her immediate post-operative care. Madame Khanh, Tuyet's aunt, and her grandmother remained at the little girl's bedside. While it was not necessary at Duong Duong that Tuyet's family provide nursing care, they did offer distraction and companionship for the little girl, and this helped the staff considerably.

Tuyet remained at Duong Duong for about two weeks, despite a quick recovery. Normally, a three- or four-day hospital stay was enough, but Khanh had other concerns. Terrorist activity and several assassination threats against Khanh posed serious security problems. He felt that his family was safer remaining temporarily at Duong Duong, rather than at their government quarters near Tan Son Nhut, five miles from Saigon, and the U.S. Embassy obliged.

Tuyet was finally discharged. The next day, we Navy nurses who provided Tuyet's care were invited to the Khanh residence. We enjoyed small delicacies, cocktails, and soft drinks served in the garden of the Khanhs' home. The general arrived late from the airport, where he had

The Khanh entourage descends upon Duong Duong.

said good-bye to U.S. Defense Secretary Robert McNamara.

Khanh impressed me as a dynamic person—and warm, friendly, and sincere when he thanked us for our care of his daughter. Madame Khanh presented us with fine Vietnamese fabric, handworked with exquisite Oriental designs.

A letter of appreciation from Prime Minister Khanh arrived several days after Tuyet's surgery:

REPUBLIC OF VIETNAM
THE PRIME MINISTER   SAIGON, March 12, 1964

Dear Captain Fisichella,

Mrs. KHANH, my daughter Tuyet, and I thank you and your staff for the wonderful courtesy and service you have shown us on the occasion of TUYET'S operation in your hospital.

I realilze that the discretion and security required inconvenienced you and probably upset the normal routine of good hospital administration. For this I apologize and beg your forgiveness.

The people of South Vietnam are well aware of the great and gracious assistance that the government and the people of the United States are rendering us in our fight for freedom and democracy. Those of you in the hospital who daily see the results of the blending of American and Vietnamese blood on the battlefield and even on the streets of Saigon are acutely aware of our problems. Rest assured that I too appreciate the gravity of the situation and the fine contribution your facility is making to our cause.

Please convey to all hands my appreciation for the fine work they are doing and my personal thanks for the courtesy and services extended my family.

Sincerely,

NGUYEN KHANH

The Khanhs remained South Vietnam's first family until 24 October 1964. On that date, the High National Council formed a civilian government and Khanh relinquished his prime minister status and became head of the armed forces in return. This represented an enormous amount of political and military maneuvering. (By 17 February 1965 he was ousted, and on 21 February, expatriated.)

TWELVE

A Frightening February

FEBRUARY MARKED the beginning of a new, terrifying phase in the war. It really began Thursday morning, 30 January 1964, when Ambassador Lodge issued a statement over Armed Forces Radio Service, indicating that potentially dangerous conditions existed in Saigon. American personnel were cautioned to stay off the streets and remain at duty stations or in quarters until further notice. It was my day off, and after breakfast I gathered my binoculars, radio, and camera equipment and headed for the roof.

I was surprised to find a sailor already there. He was breaking out a field radio. I asked what was happening, but he knew only that he had been ordered to the Ham Nghi to link up with the emergency network.

We listened intently, but heard no information. Activity in the streets below was normal. We watched and waited. I knew that armored elements and troops were in the city. That word had arrived the night before, while I was on duty. Like the news of the assassination of the chief of naval operations, this new information traveled along a grapevine that was surprisingly reliable. I expected the shooting to start at any moment.

Within an hour, the bulletin came: Condition Yellow Standby was in effect. This meant that a certain phase in the emergency plan was being activated. At 1100, a messenger from HedSuppAct delivered a sealed enveloped addressed "To the Senior Officer Present." Not only was I the senior officer present, I was the *only* officer present.

Without hesitating, I broke the seal and read the contents. My orders: I was to take command of the building, institute certain security measures, and muster available personnel. The Vietnamese building personnel were to be excluded from these procedures. Completion of the three steps satisfied Condition Yellow Standby. If Condition Yellow were activated, I was to take further action. Included in the orders:

> Determine the number of weapons and their description and the amount and description of ammunition found in the building. After making this survey, the weapons will be collected and taken to the roof in order to make a stand should it become necessary.

I mustered my personnel (two sailors). I surveyed my arsenal and listed one .22-caliber semi-automatic pistol, 100 rounds of ammunition, three Montagnard crossbows with fifty arrows and, positioned around the balustrade, eight huge potted plants. While the inclusion of potted plants seems humorous, if one was pushed from the eighth deck of the Ham Nghi and landed on a head, it would do serious damage.

For three hours, we waited. Finally, at 1400, came the news that a successful military coup d'état was complete. Gen. Nguyen Khanh, I Corps commander, had engineered the coup and replaced Gen. Duong Van Minh ("Big Minh"). Without bloodshed, General Minh, head of the Revolutionary Military Council, was arrested and removed from office.

Emergency radio operations ceased, the sailors returned to their duty stations, and Saigon life continued as usual. Most of the population was probably unaware that the government had changed hands. My three-hour command remained unique during my Navy career.

Early in February, leaflets with the message "Two Americans a Day" appeared all over Saigon. The rumor grapevine produced some alarming reports. Small poison darts shot from blow guns were aimed at the necks of Americans; Viet Cong agents were arrested carrying single-shot .45-caliber pistols resembling fountain pens; and, from a VC radio intercept, there was news of a 25,000-piaster ($150) bounty for the capture of Navy nurses. Psychological warfare had begun.

Capt. Rosario Fisichella, our new senior medical officer, was mindful of the threats and granted us permission to wear civilian clothes when we traveled to and from duty. I agreed with this decision. Keeping a low profile was the safest alternative.

Terrorist activities escalated daily. Walt Johnson invited Tweedie and me to dinner one evening at the My Canh, a floating restaurant on the Saigon River that provided a lovely setting and respite from Duong

Duong's hectic pace. We had a short walk back to the Ham Nghi. Le Loi Street was crowded with traffic and people. We passed shops, street vendors, and cafés. Suddenly, we heard the familiar, muffled sound of an explosion. A café we had passed minutes earlier blew up. We headed straight for the hospital.

Several Vietnamese civilians sustained injuries and received treatment locally. Duong Duong admitted two American GIs who had multiple wounds, which fortunately were confined to soft tissue. Neither nerve nor blood-vessel damage was elicited. The soldiers, stationed at Soc Trang in the Mekong Delta, were in Saigon on a two-day R and R. One moment they sat enjoying a cool *Ba Muoi Ba,* and the next they awoke in the Operating Room, victims of a terrorist bomb.

A gift from the café owner, a bottle of champagne tied with a big red bow, arrived during the soldiers' convalescence. They appreciated the owner's apology but told me they felt safer eating field rations with their units than dining in unpredictable Saigon. There was no warning if a terrorist attack was imminent. Other military personnel stayed away from the city.

On Sunday, 16 February, Tweedie, Flo, and I decided to see a movie at the Capitol Kinh Do Theatre. But Lt. Eileen Walsh, who had arrived in early February to replace Jan Barcott, wanted us to have dinner with her at the Brink BOQ. We accepted her invitation, since the movie at the Kinh Do was also showing the following evening.

A heavy blast rocked the Ham Nghi later that night. Window glass rattled and pictures were askew. I thought the explosion came from the area of the theater. When fire engines and ambulances, sirens screaming, headed toward the theater district, Tweedie and I left for the hospital. We expected heavy casualties.

The activity at the compound was frenetic. Litters filled the courtyard. More ambulances arrived at the gates. In the triage area, all kinds of casualties—from bruises to severe abdominal wounds—needed attention. Family members, often hysterical, milled about. They were constantly underfoot. Reporters and photographers arrived and badgered us incessantly. Investigators and military police soon pushed their way in. It was pandemonium.

Wound evaluation took priority. Lack of adequate lighting hampered the process for awhile, but portable lights solved the problem. Most of the medical staff began work in the courtyard, moving inside Duong Duong as needed.

Early in the crisis we didn't know the amount of blood needed, but there was never a shortage of fresh, whole blood. Donors arrived within minutes of learning of an explosion. The need for donors was immediately broadcast on Armed Forces Radio Service. Soldiers and sailors, responding unselfishly, knew that there could be a time when they might need blood themselves. This night was no exception. Our "walking blood bank" showed up in force and was directed to our laboratory across the street.

I reported to the Emergency and Operating rooms. Gurneys rolled in six or seven at a time. The need for gurneys was so critical that we improvised, using sawhorses to support the litters. Patients, screaming from pain, struggled with the nurses and corpsmen. I evaluated wounds, cleaned them, started IVs, stopped bleeding, took vital signs, and determined level of consciousness. I had never seen so many casualties at once, nor worked so hard to evaluate potentially critically wounded people.

I was working in the Emergency Room when one of the corpsmen arrived. He had been at the Kinh Do. The terrorist, he told me, shot the MP on duty outside the theater in cold blood. Entering the darkened auditorium, he rolled a large coffee can filled with explosives down the

The OR at Duong Duong saw extra duty during Frightening February.

A Frightening February

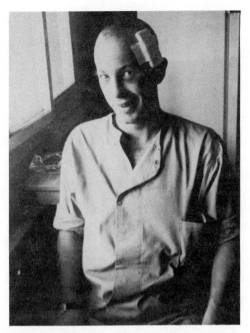

A casualty of the Capitol Kinh Do Theatre bombing, Lt. Jim Allerheiligen, suffered an eggshell fracture of the skull.

center aisle. A heroic Marine, Capt. Donald E. Koelper, saw the can and shouted for everyone to take cover. His action saved lives. Many others might have sustained blast and shrapnel injuries had they not heeded his warning.

Captain Koelper arrived at Duong Duong in critical condition. We could do little for him. The degree of brain damage was irreparable, and he died within minutes. Sixty-three people were injured, many seriously.

Military investigators told me that the rash of bombings began on 7 February. They confirmed the details provided by our corpsman and also told me that the Marine captain absorbed the primary force of the blast.

I worked my normal shift the day of the attack, stayed all night and the entire following day. By Monday, 17 February, I was exhausted from thirty-six hours of nonstop duty. I stopped by the Kinh Do Theatre after work on Tuesday. The devastation was incredible. I looked everywhere and saw twisted metal, shattered glass, huge slabs of ceiling plaster. My gaze wandered to a sight that left me limp. A cold chill ran the length of my spine.

When Tweedie and I were at the Kinh Do, we always took the same seats—on the aisle, six to ten rows from the back. This was important, because it enabled the theater staff to locate us easily if the hospital called. I now looked at those seats and realized that the explosion had occurred exactly there.

I left the theater shaken. But for a twist of fate—a last-minute decision to accept Eileen's invitation—I might not be alive. The title of the movie was *The List of Adrian Messenger*. Its plot was ironic: a bomb planted on a passenger plane detonates in midair. I left the theater. The terror I felt stayed with me for a long time.

A few days following the Kinh Do bombing, I faced cold fear again. This time I was in my quarters. Penny was on duty, Flo was out for the evening, Tweedie was taking a bath, and I was writing letters. I answered a knock at the door. Thi Ba, obviously in great distress, stood outside. A Vietnamese man I didn't recognize stood behind her. Thi Ba wept and gestured as I tried to make sense of what she was saying. The man explained, in limited English, that Thi Ba's daughter was miscarrying. Thi Ba would not be able to come tomorrow.

I absorbed the information, felt sorry for Thi Ba, but couldn't shake an unsettled feeling. Who was the man? He wasn't one of the civilian personnel employed at the Ham Nghi. I'll never know why I didn't ask him who he was. Since the beginning of that wave of terrorist strikes, my senses had been particularly sharp. Perhaps Thi Ba was participating, even unwillingly, in a ruse. Maybe the ruse involved gaining access to the seventh floor.

Thi Ba and the man left on the elevator. I was rattled, but didn't know exactly why. It all seemed so odd. Looking down, I saw a package resting against the door frame. The package was shoe-box size, wrapped in brown paper, and tied with string. A *bomb*.

The scene now made sense. I was frozen in place, literally unable to move. My mind raced with thoughts of *plastique* bombs, unremarkable packages left at strategic sites. The Ham Nghi, home to four Navy nurses and numerous other military officers, was a likely target for terrorism. I carefully shut the door but reopened it an instant later, grabbed the package, and bolted up a half-flight of stairs to the garbage chute.

If I'd used good sense, I would have run out of the building and alerted the Bomb Disposal Unit. But Tweedie languished in the tub. There wasn't time to alert her. Friendship, in a split second, superseded caution. I had to get the package to a confined area to minimize the effects of an explosion. If the blast occurred in the chute, the force would be directed vertically instead of laterally; it would be better contained.

It was too big for the chute—the darn thing stuck. I gingerly removed it. The next-best place was the stairwell behind the elevator shaft. I placed it on the deck and ran back into the quarters.

Tweedie was coming out of the head. *"Di di mau,* Tweedie," I yelled as I headed for the farthest corner of the suite. We stayed there a few moments, deciding what to do, quickly working out a plan. Tweedie left to go to the lobby to see if anyone new was at the reception desk. She planned to signal me from the street if she didn't find any strangers. I remained behind to await her signal, call the Bomb Disposal Unit, then run like hell. The assumption was that Thi Ba's and the man's appearance was a ruse, that the man was not a new employee downstairs, but a VC agent. I waited on the balcony, but there was no signal. She returned after a few minutes. There *was* a new employee at the front desk. The man told Tweedie about Thi Ba—that he had come upstairs with her to translate. It was nothing sinister.

I had to see what was in the package. Retrieving it, I poked a hole in one end, never happier to see banana skin. The box contained the day's trash. Thi Ba had left it by the door. Failing to fit it into the chute, she had decided to dispose of it on her way out, but then forgot.

It's said that if you are suddenly faced with death, your entire lifetime flashes through your mind in seconds. You couldn't prove it by me. My only thought was to put that "bomb" where it would do the least harm. I doubt that anyone has ever been more terrified than I was holding that package. As I look back twenty-eight years later, those few seconds of fear are frozen forever in my mind.

We had another "bomb" scare a week later. This time, Duong Duong's outpatient department, located across the street from the main hospital, was involved. One of our lab technicians told how a janitor, sweeping the waiting room at the end of the working day, suddenly ran pell mell into the lab. He was screaming in Vietnamese, something about the outside room. The technician walked out to the waiting room, where the janitor pointed beneath a bench to a package wrapped in brown paper. Like me, the tech froze in his tracks. But, unlike me, he recovered quickly, cleared the building, and called the Bomb Disposal Unit.

Standing outside the door, the tech saw the BDU man carefully examine the package. He emerged a few minutes later carrying the "bomb" and wearing a sheepish grin. It was a box of sanitary napkins apparently left by a patient. We were razzed for weeks afterward about the "Kotex bomb." The story was widely circulated in Saigon, and I heard that it made *Stars and Stripes*.

Terrorist incidents increasingly restricted our activities in the city. The Kinh Do was rebuilt, but movies were no longer shown to Americans. As a matter of fact, gatherings of Americans were avoided. The popular USO photo tours stopped. This was particularly disappointing to me, so I organized impromptu classes and photo safaris for our corpsmen. Four or five of us headed out on Saturday mornings to take photos. We poked around the Saigon back streets or along the Cholon canals. The safaris were risky—we were off the beaten track.

The USO presented a prime terrorist target. Precautions taken to protect American personnel were in place by the end of February. Because the building front was plate glass, it was sandbagged. Inside the main entrance, a sandbag tunnel with a 90-degree turn was built and draped with a bright orange-and-white parachute to alleviate the drab appearance. It looked like something out of the World War II London blitz, when similar "decorations" were employed.

February was a hellish month. The "Two Americans a Day" threat weighed heavily on us. At least in the realm of psychological warfare, the VC had scored a few points.

THIRTEEN

Singapore and More

WHILE LIBERTY WEEKENDS to Da Lat and Cambodia were brief and refreshing respites, I came to sense the need for a real rest, a vacation, and the rehabilitation part of R and R. All military personnel were granted a ten-day R and R leave of absence during the Vietnam War. There were many ways to spend leave—trips to Hawaii or Japan were popular—but I chose to take two five-day leaves, one to Bangkok and one to Hong Kong.

A January cholera epidemic in Saigon almost nixed the Bangkok trip, but fortunately the staff at Duong Duong got enough people vaccinated. Betty Murphy, the Saigon USO director, Tweedie, and I took off with about sixty other American personnel.

That night we ate dinner at a fabulous outdoor Hungarian restaurant, where torches burned softly and stolling musicians played gypsy tunes. In this setting, we could finally relax and unwind. For the first time, we were without fear of a terrorist grenade flying over the garden wall. For a time, we could let our guard down. We were acutely aware of the mental freedom.

Bangkok is described as the Venice of Asia because of its many *klongs*, or canals. One day we boarded a motor launch before sunrise and set out on the Floating Market Tour. We were a flotilla of four or five launches heading down the Chao Phraya River. *Klongs* branched off the river, alive with a community of water people. *Klong*-dwellers, like the Saigon River people, complete the life cycle afloat. We plied the waterways for five hours, passing under canopies of thick foliage, a backdrop for brightly colored birds and exotic flowers. Monkeys chattered at us.

Along the *klongs* of Bangkok, the "Venice of Asia"

And floating vendors, seemingly by the dozens, hawked everything from coffee to furniture.

A silk-factory tour completed our cruise. Impressed by the bolts of shimmering fabric that had been dyed and woven by Thai artisans, I bought yards of it for gifts. The owner of the factory was Jim Thompson, a mysterious American businessman. A local legend, Jim eventually disappeared under cryptic circumstances. He stepped outside a mountain retreat in the Cameron Highlands and was never seen again. I still wonder if he was involved with the intelligence community.

A legend of a different sort was Johny of the Johny Gems jewelry store, where American personnel were offered the best prices on fine jewelry, teak carvings, and bronze flatware. I was especially taken by gold rings set with black and blue star sapphires and smoky topaz. One morning, Johny sent a car to take us to tour his bronze-ware factory outside Bangkok. It was a large open-air pavilion with a dirt deck and primitive forge. Shaping and grinding of the bronze was done by hand; rosewood or buffalo-horn flatware handles were carved by craftsmen

Thailand's temples were incomparable.

squatting on the deck. Though the techniques were crude, the products were exquisite.

Sightseeing in Bangkok may be one of those experiences difficult to duplicate elsewhere. My camera snapped endlessly as I captured the Thai sun glinting off the golden roofs of the temples with distinctive names—the Temple of the Emerald Buddha, the Temples of the Reclining Buddha, Temple Benchamabobitr (meaning the temple constructed by the fifth king of the dynasty; it housed an exquisite gallery of fifty ancient images of Lord Buddha, all cast in bronze). I tried to preserve on film and in memory the massive architecture, the tiled pagodas along the riverbanks, the brilliant colors.

In Hong Kong, where Tweedie and I joined Florence and John Web, who was stationed in Da Nang as adviser to the U.S. Operations Mission, we stayed at the Park Hotel in Kowloon City, on the Chinese mainland. Five cents bought a ride on the Star Ferry from the mainland to Hong Kong. The Kowloon Train Station was nearby. It fascinated me to know that from that station, I could begin a journey to Paris on the fabled Ori-

Aged and young beggars at the border to Communist China

ent Express. A tram carried us to Victoria Peak, where we took in spectacular views of the harbor, the city of Hong Kong, Repulse Bay (famous as the site of the English surrender to the Japanese, as immortalized in James Clavell's *Brother Rat*), the charming Tiger Balm Gardens, and Aberdeen Fishing Village. At dusk, dinner on the twenty-fifth floor of the Hong Kong Hilton gave us a panoramic view of the colony, with twinkling lights gradually turning on.

A trip to the Red Chinese border was, naturally, on the itinerary. The coastal road twisted through rugged terrain and around inlets and coves, where two big Red Chinese seagoing junks were anchored close to shore.

The Loc Ma Chau Police Station, just a half mile from the border, offered the best view of Communist China. The village and countryside across the border appeared bleak and austere. It felt strange to be looking at the Bamboo Curtain that separated Communist and non-Communist China. Canton, Chungking, Shanghai, and Peking lay beyond the misty purple hills. These fabulous cities once housed the magnificent riches and culture of great dynasties. Their gates provided the terminal points for huge caravans traversing the vast expanse of old China. Kublai Khan once stopped in a rocky, secluded valley outside Peking, scratching into a stone wall "Kublai Khan, for whom the world was made." Modern-day politics had made these treasures inaccessible to us.

American military personnel were discouraged from visiting Macau, a Portuguese island colony. Macau, with its rich green countryside, was the Garden City of the Orient. But Red Chinese patrol boats kept close watch on Chinese defectors who tried to swim to freedom. Macau, where defectors were shot in mid-swim, could be dangerous.

A problem with their passports prevented John and Florence from taking the trip, but Tweedie and I enjoyed a full day of sightseeing. The tour guide showed us the Red Chinese Library and two schools—one flying the Red Chinese flag, the other the Portuguese flag. A fireworks cottage industry flourished on Macau's back streets. I saw a 105-year-old Chinese woman constructing firecrackers. She loved to pose for the cameras.

We visited two of Macau's famous gambling dens. The den inside a floating houseboat was my favorite. Fan-tan and mahjong were favorite games. Tweedie and I were barred from entering the side and back rooms; we never learned why. The hydrofoil *Flying Phoenix* returned us to Hong Kong, just ahead of a nasty storm blowing out from the mainland.

A 105-year-old firecracker maker

Most of the last day of our Hong Kong R and R was spent in the local police station and the American Consulate. Tweedie's wallet, containing her passport, had been stolen in Thieves Market, our first and last stop. Tweedie was asked to recreate the incident by a Hong Kong police detective. He interviewed nearby shop owners to no avail. The detective called the American consulate from the police station and reported the passport theft, then issued a *laissez-passer*, a temporary passport. There was a good chance the papers would turn up, he told Tweedie. Sure enough, ten days after our return to Saigon, the consulate called. A package had arrived from Hong Kong via courier. The detective's prediction proved true. Tweedie and her papers were reunited. Even if they had not been, we had had a marvelous five days in Hong Kong.

Our March Singapore liberty was wedged in between the two R and Rs. That February in Saigon had been the pits. We had treated the Kinh Do Theatre bombing victims, attended to the soldiers wounded in the café on Le Loi Street, and survived a couple of scary false alarms. We had hoped that the Singapore trip would be a welcome return to normalcy, even though stability was eroding there too. But it was now or never if I was to visit Malaysia.

I was given liberty for the weekend plus the entire Friday. Tweedie and I departed from Tan Son Nhut after work Thursday evening. The lovely Merlin Hotel in Kuala Lumpur, 250 miles north of Singapore, was our first overnight stop. Friday morning, we hired a car and driver and began to explore. Kuala Lumpur was a modern, energetic city. We drove past zoological gardens, the attractive university campus, and a meticulously maintained country club with greens, fairways, and tennis courts. A highlight was a visit to the city's sports arena, with its brilliant colors and Oriental decor, one of the most unusual stadiums in the world.

Outside the Kuala Lumpur city limits, the jungle thickened into nearly solid green walls. Native huts appeared where trails cut through the primitive jungle. Water buffalo and livestock grazed alongside the trails as we headed toward the Batu Caves. These caves were honeycombed in four-hundred-foot-tall limestone cliffs. I ventured up the many steps carved into a cliff to explore the largest cave, awesomely huge and with echoes of past religious significance.

The next stop was a sprawling rubber plantation. I remember the sun directly overhead and scorching hot. The leaves of the rubber trees spared us sunstroke as we watched native tappers at work collecting the raw, sticky white latex in small metal crucibles. Since the death of the tree resulted if the incision in the tree bark was not precise, this was a surgical procedure of another kind.

Somerset Maugham once wrote that the Raffles hotel in Singapore stood "for all the fables of the exotic East." Arriving there Friday afternoon, we found that Somerset Maugham had not exaggerated. The Raffles was a classic example of one of the great old colonial hotels. The remainder of our first hot night in Singapore was spent sipping iced quinine water on the Raffles' spectacular veranda.

A pedaled tri-sha took us on a tour of Singapore Saturday morning. On narrow, eerie Sago Lane, lined with drab buildings, we looked at an opium den. We visited a Death House further along the street. Old Chinese people, responding to a unique premonition of impending death, enter these houses to die. They give whatever money they have to the young Chinese girls who staff the house to attend to the old people's every need. It was a sad and depressing sight to see the aged quietly lying on benches, waiting for the end. Looking back on this, though, I wonder if it wasn't a forerunner of the hospice.

The waterfront was as colorful as it was malodorous. One stevedore

I encountered resembled a character from the *Terry and the Pirates* comic strip. I'll never forget him. He chewed betel nut with a set of rotten, discolored teeth, and dressed in stereotypical pirate's clothing complete with a red bandana, a black patch covering one eye, and an eight-inch kris inside a sheath. I was in the haunt of the much-storied Malay river pirates.

The last time we had been in a department store was six months earlier in San Francisco. At Singapore's C. K. Tang Department Store, we were agog at the wonderful items from all over the world, for sale at good prices. American cosmetics were available cheaper than in the States.

Happily motoring on the river Saturday evening, we were oblivious to a rapidly disintegrating political climate. A delightful, elderly tour group dined with us in the Raffles dining room after the cruise. At 2230 we retired to our rooms. Forty-five mintues later, I was catapulted from my sleep and from my bed. A bomb had exploded outside the hotel. The blast was unmistakable. I had been living through the same explosions for months in Saigon. What irony: seventy-two hours of liberty, six hundred miles from Saigon, and still there was no escaping the brutality of terrorism. Four rooms were blown in. The Raffles sustained severe damage, but fortunately, no one was injured.

We arrived at the Ham Nghi in Saigon at 1200 on Sunday. Ann Richman wasted no time updating us. The biggest flash, literally, was a Viet Cong attempt to blow up MAAG headquarters. A Vietnamese employee had been caught red-handed attempting to smuggle an explosive charge into the building. The timer had been set to detonate Saturday morning just when staff reported for duty. The results, had the terrorist not been caught, would have been devastating.

With Ann's story and our own Singapore experience, it seemed as though we had never been away. The *Stars and Stripes* had this to say:

> Still another spy told us the case of the double-bombed nurses. The Navy nurses worked feverishly and long (and, we're sorry, without any credit at all!) during the rash of February bombings in Saigon, helping patch up victims in the Station Hospital. So, for a little rest and recreation, a couple of them took off for a well-earned, brief vacation in Singapore. Well, first thing that happened was that the hotel in which they were staying . . . ah, you guessed it. That's right, the hotel was bombed.

FOURTEEN

Season of Sacrifice

IT WAS 29 MARCH 1964—Easter. Precautions stemming from the un-relenting terrorist attacks that were, more than ever, targeting Americans moved the Easter sunrise service to the rooftop area of a Bachelor Officers' Quarters in downtown Saigon. Vicious terrorist attacks were most successful at ground level—in cafés or outdoors—so it was decided to forgo a riverfront service. The lessons learned at the Pershing Field explosion and the Kinh Do Theatre provided an ongoing education in understanding the guerrilla terrorist mentality. Better management of the safety of Americans resulted.

Easter morning was cool and sparkling clear. It was a typical equatorial sunrise. The sun seemingly rose out of the river in spectacular fashion, bathing the city in an instantaneous flash of light. Missing was that half-light, predawn period that we in the Northern Hemisphere are accustomed to. The peculiar, sudden onset of both morning light and sudden darkness no longer captivated me—I was accustomed to it.

The previous year's sunrise service came to mind. I was stationed at Quantico, Virginia, where the service was held on the shore of the Potomac River. That Easter morning was also clear and beautiful. There was a heavy, crisp frost and a frigid wind off the Potomac, which nearly caused frostbite. There was no possibility of frostbite in tropical Saigon.

The congregation beheld a commanding view of the city, the Saigon River, and the battle-scarred countryside beyond as it listened to the chaplain's words. But I was aware of an irony. The spires of the Saigon Cathedral were prominent on the landscape a short distance away. Inside the cathedral, I imagined, Catholic Vietnamese were worshiping Christ's resurrection, as we were. While the Vietnamese worshiped freely in relative safety, we, dedicated to the protection of these people and their right to religious freedom, found ourselves subjugated by political and military limitations.

It was a deceiving scene, a facade of peace and serenity. The sight and sound of artillery shells arching over the same countryside could in a moment shatter the pseudoserenity, mortar and small-arms rounds joining larger projectiles in their flight to target. Magnesium flares could turn night into day as they dropped over the area under attack.

This was Vietnam on Easter morning, 1964. Serene and inspiring, it was concurrently sinister and treacherous. Its strangeness provided the observer, as always, with a fascinating study in contrasts.

Fighting had escalated in all sectors around Saigon by Easter. There were more casualties: gunshot and shrapnel wounds and punji-stick victims. These latter were liable to develop severe, rapid infection of the foot; punji sticks were sharpened bamboo, fire-hardened and dipped in excrement (which was highly toxic), and so sharp they could penetrate combat boots. There were survivors and there were those who ultimately succumbed to their injuries. At times, our hospital overflowed with injured.

The OR lights often burned late into the night during April. We worked hard to deal with the pressures of a rapidly building war. Tweedie especially worked long and difficult hours. She was our only anesthetist, the only nurse trained to administer anesthetic drugs. These drugs enabled the surgeons to suture wounds, amputate limbs, set fractures, and manage the other surgical procedures found in a combat-casualty hospital.

The night sky viewed from our Ham Nghi balcony provided a surrealistic sight. The pyrotechnics of war—the orange muzzle flash of artillery, red and green streaks from tracer ammunition, and the intense white light of magnesium flares—illuminated the countryside. Palm trees on the opposite side of the Saigon River were silhouetted against blackness as parachute flares drifted downward. The display was awesome.

The details of the night of 4 April are indelibly stamped in my mind. It was Saturday evening. Our new Senior Medical Officer, Capt. Rosario Fisichella, and his wife arrived for a welcome dinner of fried chicken and all the fixings. Ann, Tweedie, and I looked forward to entertaining.

Just as we began eating, the officer of the day called to alert us to an inbound "dust-off." We left for the hospital in a hurry, heading through

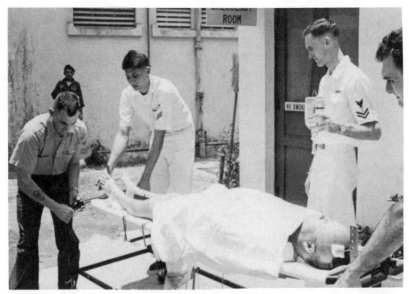

A quadriplegic patient being readied for transport to Clark Air Force Base Hospital

heavy city traffic. The "dust-off" arrived at the nearby soccer field. Ambulances met the chopper and received the wounded, arriving at the hospital at the same time we did.

A quick evaluation of the injured men by doctors, nurses, and corpsmen was handled in the Emergency Room. A dozen combat casualties arrived, extending the perimeters of the Emergency Room to include the courtyard. One casualty, an Army captain, suffered a critical neck wound of the cervical spine with resultant quadriplegia. He was in shock but somewhat lucid. While exploring and debriding his wound, we treated his shock with intravenous fluids and whole blood to stabilize his condition. We conducted a standard neurological exam to determine sensation loss in his extremities. He probably would remain quadriplegic the rest of his life. His career had been abruptly halted in the fantastically short time it took a sniper's bullet to pass through the captain's neck. At best, he would spend the rest of his life confined to a wheelchair. The captain stayed at our hospital for only a short time; our emergency treatment prepared him for the four-and-a-half-hour flight to Clark Air Force Base Hospital.

Another young man, a helicopter pilot, still dressed in his olive-drab flight suit and wearing a flak jacket, lay on a nearby stretcher. Flak jackets provide "armor" against most small-arms fire. The jacket, this time, had been useless.

There was no pulse when I pressed my fingers against the carotid artery. His eyes were glazed, pupils fixed. Unzipping his jacket, I saw that two bullets had penetrated and entered his anterior chest wall. His flight suit was blood-soaked. Chest examination revealed massive bone and soft-tissue damage.

When I removed the flak jacket, blood gushed from his wounds, splashing me and pooling under the stretcher. I examined the exit wounds of the posterior chest. The entire posterior chest wall was blown away by bullets, probably .45 or .50 caliber.

Examining his personal effects was the only thing left to do. In his wallet I discovered a photo of a young woman standing with two tiny toddlers. The little girls were as pretty as their mother. In the courtyard chaos, I stood beside this young man, a warrant officer only twenty-four years old. Gazing for a moment at the photograph, I then turned my attention to him. I reached down and held his hand. It was cooling, his fingers stiffening. I looked at that young, handsome face, and tears filled my eyes. I am certain that procedure was followed and the photo and other effects were turned over to the morgue detail. I, however, have no memory of it. And, strangely, I didn't share the experience with Walt, Ann, Tweedie, or the others.

Since then, I have wondered what triggered my unusual reaction. It was our habit to return to quarters, unwind, and discuss the injuries and the patients. Perhaps, after discovering the photo, I wanted somehow to protect this young man's privacy, choosing not to discuss the details. It was a singular incident, never repeated during my tour.

These young men had been coming through our Operating Room doors for seven months. Some never reached the doors. Each was becoming more difficult to accept. I had reached a saturation point that day. When would it end? These casualties were among the best of our young soldiers, volunteers who had chosen to serve in Vietnam. Some gave their young lives on a remote, foreign soil for reasons too complex for many to understand.

I could not indulge in depressing thoughts. Work remained to be done. There were others to treat, to admit, and to help settle into their beds that night. The word *settle* may seem an odd choice, but it is not. These men came from chaos. They were wounded, lifted filthy from a muddy rice paddy, medevaced, and treated, emerging from all this confusion and pain to finally settle between clean white sheets.

We returned to our quarters sometime on the far side of midnight. We ate cold chicken and fell exhausted into bed. It was the end of another day at Duong Duong. These days were in themselves miniature dramas. And these dramas unfolded increasingly frequently at U.S. Naval Station Hospital, Saigon.

The next weekend was even worse. I started dinner on Friday, 10 April, and didn't return for another meal until Monday. I was on duty for thirty-six continuous hours, first in the Recovery Room, then in the Operating Room, then returning to the Recovery Room. The weekend battle, possibly in the Mekong Delta, resulted in two DOAs and thirteen casualties. We treated many multiple-gunshot and shrapnel wounds, most of the wounds severe.

The activity let up on Monday. There was a chance to recover my energy before the next crisis occurred. A good hot meal, shower and shampoo, and a nice long sleep revived me.

An unprecedented tragedy occurred a day or two later. The tail boom of a helicopter broke off in flight. It had not been shot off, nor had there been a midair collision. Several ARVN soldiers fell to their deaths. Three U.S. crew members were also killed in the crash. Our hospital received the only survivor, a soldier with burns over 50 percent of his body.

These episodes came at a time when Saigon was scorching. Temperatures soared to 98 degrees in the shade and 120 degrees on the streets. It was the prelude to the monsoon season. Because military field operations were difficult to mount in downpours, mud, and floods, there was a substantial increase in fighting (and casualties) just prior to each monsoon.

The season of sacrifice was not over, however. There was another sacrifice, occurring on the eve of the monsoon.

May Day is 1 May. It has held particular significance for the Communist world ever since 1889, when the Second Socialist International designated the spring holiday as the celebration of labor. The U.S. Embassy issued bulletins to the American community in Saigon—we were cautioned to remain alert to any kind of VC terrorist activity. These activities were expected in the city: such attacks were a favored mode of celebration. But since the nature of terrorism lies in its unpredictability, we expected the attack in some bizarre form.

The monsoon season was preceded by a month or so of severe, violent thunderstorms. These storms rarely brought rain. Wicked bolts of lightning sizzled down from masses of angry, black clouds. Often a bolt struck something and exploded with the ferocity of a 155-mm artillery shell. Sometimes it was hard to distinguish between the heavenly wrought explosions and those created by the ongoing conflict.

Just before sunrise on 2 May, the city was rocked by another blast. Lightning storms had been particularly wicked at night. It was a noise among many noises, and we attached no particular significance to the sound. We soon learned that it represented the VC blowing up the USNS *Card,* moored on the river at the Saigon Harbor, not far from our quarters. Fortunately, her mooring lines were immediatley snugged up to prevent capsize. With a water level of just forty-eight feet, the ship settled to the bottom upright. Some of its superstructure remained visible.

Although damage was considerable both to the cargo and to the ship's hull, there were no casualties.

At this point in the conflict, U.S. ships had seemed immune to attack. Suddenly, they appeared vulnerable. Something bizarre had joined the vast company of the expected. The sinking of the *Card* dealt a terrible blow to morale as well as to American prestige. Vietnamese citizens, who perceived us as their protectors, had good reason to take pause. The sinking had great propaganda value. The *Card,* transferred by the Navy to be operated by merchant seamen, was one of the smaller types of aircraft carrier. Her primary mission was the transporting of aircraft and helicopters to Vietnam. We hadn't lost a carrier to hostile attack since World War II. Eventually, the ship was salvaged. While no casualties resulted from the attack on the *Card,* later, on the evening of 2 May, we had plenty of injured to deal with.

Large crowds visited the waterfront to view the ship. The *My Canh* was moored nearby. A group of newly arrived soldiers observed the ship, then boarded the *My Canh* for dinner. They left the restaurant and crossed the street. Some of the men had been in country for just three days—not long enough to develop that inner alertness or "double vision," as Col. Robert B. Rigg called it in his book *How To Stay Alive in Vietnam.*

There was a sudden, blinding flash. The flash was followed by the explosion of a grenade detonated in their midst. Where there had just been eight young men (sobered no doubt from their viewing of the *Card*) walking along a pleasant tree-lined street, there were now eight writhing, bleeding terrorist victims lying in a dirty gutter and crying out in pain. We worked far into the night cleaning, debriding, suturing, packing, and dressing multiple shrapnel wounds. Some of the victims sustained severe blast injuries to the eyes.

The attack was characterized by a favored VC tactic. A bicyclist rode past the group and dropped an activated grenade through a hole in his pants pocket. It rolled down the inside of his pants leg onto the street. The bicycle was ideal for a speedy escape through the gathering crowd —the terrorist never was apprehended.

A season of sacrifice came to a traumatic and unsettled conclusion. The ever-increasing casualties taxed both our physical and emotional resources. I noted ironies that characterized for me the strangeness of this war. A general would conduct a day's battle and then return home for an evening of bridge. A soldier could hop a supply chopper and pass a day off from the war on a beach. Was combat here like a day at the office?

I bicycled down Tu Do Street shortly after Easter and sat in the shade of a palm tree on the river's edge. Such solitary escapes provided, for me, an opportunity for reflection. I was comforted by the sight of a water scene, which offered a sense of peace and tranquillity. In those unsettled and troubled days, I made many trips to the river. I had a need for the solace and comfort these trips provided. As I write these words, I realize that this is a moment of true serendipity: *Tranquillity, Solace,* and *Comfort* were the names of three U.S. Navy hospital ships.

FIFTEEN
Salutes

THE NAVY NURSE CORPS celebrated its fifty-sixth anniversary on 13 May 1964. The anniversary of the Corps is celebrated by Navy nurses all over the world, and our senior nurse, Ann Richman, decided to have a tea on the Rex BOQ roof. We worried that the weather would interfere, since it was the monsoon season. Sure enough, at 1500 on 13 May, the wind swept in, the heavens opened, and the season's first monsoon was upon us. Decorations and flowers sailed over the side. Hairdos went limp. Our dress whites were soaked. Somehow, we salvaged the gorgeous blue-and-gold cake. Twenty minutes later, the sun sparkled and the streets dried. Despite the monsoon, our anniversary party wasn't scuttled.

Later in the week, and in observance of our anniversary, I treated myself to a new Nikon 35-mm camera. The Saturday after the party, Tweedie and I boarded a *cyclo* and headed for the Saigon Zoo and Botanical Gardens, where there would be plenty of opportunity to try out my new Nikon. We'd only been there an hour when suddenly a corpsman from Duong Duong appeared.

Dr. Johnson needed us immediately, he explained. An emergency medevac was arriving. We hurried back to the OR. The corpsman had briefed us on the basics of the case—a severe hand injury.

An Army captain flying a helicopter combat-support mission had sustained the injury when a grenade prematurely detonated. His crew spotted Viet Cong activity on the ground and began dropping white phosphorus grenades to mark the location. The grenades' thick white smoke made an easier target for planes called in on an air strike.

Our patient pulled the pin on a grenade that exploded before he dropped it, his right hand receiving the full force of the blast. He sustained not only the blast effect in his hand, but also had burning, white phosphorus particles blown deeply into the remaining hand tissue. These casualties present a unique problem, because the injured tissue retains particles of phosphorus. The particles, when exposed to air, continue to smolder and burn deep within the wound. Toxic phosphorus, absorbed by the body, further complicates the injury. Death may result if sufficient quantities are absorbed.

Treating this casualty was tricky. I immersed his hand in a weak copper sulfate solution. The copper sulfate reacted with the phosphorus, forming a coating around the particles. Using forceps, Walt removed them.

A portion of the hand needed to be amputated. Walt saw my camera and asked me to photograph the hand from several angles. Walt wanted a record of the injury, because occasionally an amputee attempts legal action, thinking the amputation wasn't necessary.

Walt continued to debride the wound. Some particles continued smoldering. I repeated the soaking procedure, wary that there was a potential for copper sulfate toxicity. With each application, we became more apprehensive. I watched for signs such as kidney damage and hemolysis (breakdown of the red blood cells). Worse, hemolysis is intensified by the ingestion of the antimalarial drugs taken by all personnel in Vietnam.

Walt closed the case but warned us that he thought more particles would ignite within twenty-four hours. Several hours later, I saw the soldier's pressure dressing smoke. He returned to surgery, where we repeated the procedures of soaking and debriding. Walt removed more particles and excised necrotic tissue. Although Walt Johnson was neither a hand specialist nor a plastic surgeon, that case was the finest surgery I saw in Vietnam. Only the thumb and part of the index finger were amputated.

The soldier was free of all effects from copper sulfate and phosphorus poisoning when he was medevaced several days later. We were the initiating hospital, and we never learned of cases' outcomes unless patients notified us of their recoveries. We were all curious about the final outcome of the hand surgery, but unfortunately we never heard from the soldier again.

In June, the monsoon season came with a vengeance. The downpours came off and on all day. One Tuesday night, we watched an intense

The Navy Nurse Corps anniversary photo: left to right, Lt. Carleda Lorberg; Lt. Comdr. Tweedie Searcy; Lt. Comdr. Bobbi Hovis; Capt. Malcolm Friedman; Comdr. Ann Richman, senior nurse; Lt. Eileen Walsh; Lt. (jg) Darby Reynolds; Capt. Rosario Fisichella

firefight rage several miles from our balcony. Viet Cong were attacking a hamlet outside Saigon. We heard firing and saw muzzle flashes between flare drops. The fighting was intense, and we expected casualties. Morning came, and we had not received a phone call all night. It was unusual. The battle still raged. I watched it from the balcony until I left for work.

No casualties arrived during my shift, but we did receive a "dust-off" alert that a soldier was coming in. Tweedie, the P.M. nurse, and I waited for word that the chopper had arrived. The evening wore on, but no call came. Where was the casualty? we wondered. Word arrived that ground fire was so heavy that attempting to medevac the soldier was suicide. The ground fire was bad enough, but the severe weather made attempting a rescue an even worse risk.

It troubled me. Somewhere in the firefight, a wounded soldier lay awaiting rescue. Nothing worked in his favor: the capability to rescue him, transport him, and probably save his life was there, but the intensity of the battle and the monsoon interfered.

Soldiers in all wars die under tragic circumstances. These tragic circumstances were unique, and they were particularly frustrating. President John F. Kennedy addressed the U.S. Naval Academy graduating class of 1962 and said:

> You fight another kind of war—new in its intensity, ancient in its origin—war by guerrillas, subversives, insurgents, assassins, war by ambush instead of by combat, by infiltration instead of aggression, seeking victory by eroding and exhausting the enemy instead of engaging him.

The next morning, we learned that the soldier had died. He was an adviser—a volunteer soldier advising an ARVN unit. He survived long enough to warrant a call for rescue. But no rescue came.

Our troops displayed remarkable endurance and adaptability. They lived often on fish and rice or whatever they could scrounge. Paddy water treated with halogen tablets replaced fresh drinking water. Their clothes were seldom dry. Insects and leeches attacked them with great ferocity.

Daytime heat was steamy and stifling. At night, they chilled to the bone. They slept in swamps, paddies, or jungles, even during monsoons. Daily, they confronted the unpredictability of the enemy. Ambush and capture could occur at any moment, or a firefight could break out. Rescue was often difficult, but somehow many soldiers survived the odds. No wonder they expressed their gratitude for the "luxuries" of clean beds, showers, and hot food.

We received a "dust-off" call late one afternoon. The soldier arrived, eighteen years old, blond hair, blue eyes. He was lifted from the stretcher onto the Emergency Room table. Sammy's fatigues were soaked in mud and paddy water—so were his wounds.

I began cutting away his fatigues. Walt examined him. Sammy shivered from mild hypothermia, though the outside temperature was in the nineties. He sustained multiple shrapnel injuries. Sammy told me his story as I scrubbed his wounds.

He had been on patrol in the Mekong Delta. It was night, and the patrol encountered a Viet Cong unit. The patrol members became separated when the fighting broke out. Sammy was wounded and suddenly alone. He rolled down the side of a rice-paddy dike, submerging himself in muddy water.

Minutes ticked away like hours. He wondered if he would see the sunrise. "Unfriendly fire" surrounded him throughout the night as he lay there in pain. But Sammy was lucky—friendly forces found him the following morning.

I worked to make Sammy comfortable. Warm blankets covered him, a deterrent to hypothermia.

"Ma'am, do you know what it means to see a pretty American nurse in a clean, white uniform?" Sammy asked while timidly holding my hand. "And to be cared for in your hospital?"

Tears filled his eyes. Mine, too. I couldn't say anything. I squeezed his hand instead. I slid his arm under the blankets and tucked the blankets under his chin. Sammy defied the odds. Unlike the unknown soldier who died before he could reach us, Sammy survived. Blood loss, shock, hypothermia, and septicemia—blood poisoning—confronted him. We treated him with heavy doses of antibiotics. Waiting and administering routine care was all that we could do.

For three weeks Sammy stayed at Duong Duong, where he received a Purple Heart. He couldn't do enough to help us, once he was permitted out of bed. He carried trays, fed patients, assisted in squaring away the wards, and performed other minor but necessary details. Sammy was our hospital "pet" and morale booster. If a patient felt sorry for himself or behaved obnoxiously, we sent Sammy. He was a pretty good amateur psychologist.

The war followed Sammy to Duong Duong. A severe blast rocked the hospital one morning when a bomb detonated on a sidewalk nearby. The Bomb Disposal Unit reported that it was a crudely designed device. When the timer was set off accidentally, the bomb was hastily abandoned. Only part of the charge exploded. It was a thirty-pound bomb, big enough to do severe damage. The BDU felt that it was meant for us.

Finally, Sammy returned to full duty. He dropped by Duong Duong one last time, a few weeks later. He was doing just fine the last time I saw him. To steal a line from Barry Sadler's "Ballad of the Green Berets," "These are men, America's best."

While participating in the Korean airlift, I had wanted to visit Corregidor and see the site of the underground hospital there, but I never had the opportunity. During the summer of my Saigon tour, I finally saw for myself evidence of the bravery and sacrifice of Navy nurses—other examples of America's best.

During World War II, the United States Army established a hospital underground on the fortress island of Corregidor. Corregidor was the

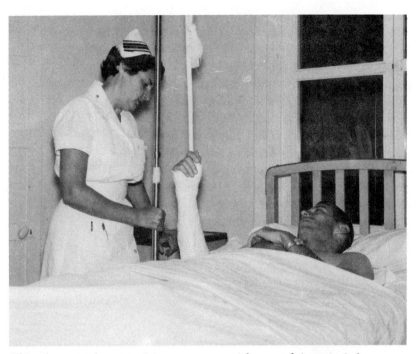

This photograph, capturing a moment with one of America's best, appeared in *Stars and Stripes*.

most famous of the 7,000 Philippine Islands because of its unique role during the early days of World War II. It was the site of the last-ditch stand by Filipino and American armies against the invading Japanese in May 1942. During the surrender of Filipino and American forces, eleven U.S. Navy nurses were captured and remained POWs for three years.

Corregidor is a small, tadpole-shaped island at the mouth of Manila Bay. It is only three miles long, rocky, and covered with thick jungle growth. When aerial attacks on Corregidor began, all American military units moved underground beneath Malinta Hill. Miles of tunnels and spaces had been excavated in preparation for such an eventuality. The fortress held for five months.

Tweedie and I caught a ride on a Navy medevac flight to Clark AFB, overnighted there, then motored to Manila the next day. A hydrofoil boat carried us across Manila Bay to Corregidor.

We arrived and followed a walking tour across the island. On Malinta Hill the surface buildings were reduced to rubble. Only steel girders and some concrete remained of the original Army hospital. Most of the gun batteries were rusted and overgrown with jungle growth. I was surprised to find a few that were still in good condition.

We entered the underground hospital by walking down a stone ramp. Remnants of the original hospital equipment remained, and we could identify wards carved out of solid rock formations. The rooms were dim and dank: a string of wire with bare light bulbs suspended provided the only light. The nurses' quarters were dungeon-like. Water seeped through the walls. Rusting metal tables and beds, army cots with torn canvas, and broken wooden bedside lockers had been left behind by the Japanese.

I tried to imagine what it was like, nursing during daily Japanese bombing attacks. And knowing that it was only a matter of time before the Japanese surrendered. I knew the stories of the eleven Navy nurses and knew how much they and their Army sisters feared capture by the Japanese. Both Corregidor and Bataan are national shrines, fittingly in honor of those who died defending the "Rock."

SIXTEEN

Flight Line

I OWNED AN AIRPLANE before I owned a car, so it was not surprising that aviation was for me an important part of my tour in Vietnam. I had taken one step after another toward my career goals, and several of those steps focused on flying. They had all helped lead me to this billet.

Early opportunities came through the Civilian Defense Program, where reserve military were teachers. The program offered aviation ground-school training, which I completed in 1943 while a senior at Edinboro High School. My Navy career goals became Flight Nursing, Aviation Medicine, and Medical Air Evacuation. Since there was no gasoline during World War II, I had to postpone getting air time, but I earned my pilot's wings in 1948 (my flight instructor ceremonially and literally cut the tail off my shirt after my first solo); I was an ensign then, stationed at Jacksonville Naval Air Station Hospital in Florida.

I bought a Piper Cub, J-3, instead of a car while I was stationed at Key West Naval Hospital. After the Korean War, in 1953, my duty station was Quonset Point Naval Air Station, Rhode Island. The lieutenant I was dating flew an F3D Sky Night jet aircraft. We boarded the F3D one morning for a training flight. I took the right-hand seat. A large toggle-type switch was between the seats, allowing me to have full aileron control of the jet. I could change the direction of the aircraft and roll it, and for a thrilling half hour I flew an F3D—climbing, banking, and descending. It was probably the first time a female member of the Navy flew a Navy jet.

I saw a lot of flight-line action during my Saigon duty. Duong Duong's second patient after commissioning—the soldier with carbuncles—

returned to the hospital in February suffering from a hot, infected knee. He was admitted with a high fever, knee-joint involvement, and appeared systemically ill. He did not respond to antibiotic treatment, and his condition rapidly deteriorated. The ward medical officer decided that the soldier required immediate medical air evacuation to a larger, more sophisticated facility.

Routine medevac flights departed Saigon on Tuesdays and Fridays for the Medevac Detachment Headquarters at Clark Air Force Base in the Philippines. The soldier's condition worsened after the routine Tuesday flight had departed. We did not think he could survive until the Friday flight, so we notified Clark AFB and requested an emergency medevac for the following A.M.

Air Force Flight Nurse Capt. Virginia Armstrong and her medical technicians coordinated all medevac missions operating in Southeast Asia. Captain Armstrong arrived at Clark AFB just as our urgent request was received. Coincidentally, a C-130 was on the flight line turning up for a mission to Tachikawa, Japan. The flight was diverted and, with Captain Armstrong aboard, headed for Saigon. Captain Fisichella gave me TAD (temporary additional duty) orders to accompany the sick soldier on the emergency flight.

Aboard the C-130, Virginia and I made the patient comfortable. In flight, we kept an IV running and checked his level of consciousness, vital signs, and his urinary output. He was semiconscious and somewhat disoriented. He withstood the flight but developed symptoms of renal failure, a condition that contributed to his disorientation. Disorientation is caused by a severe blood chemistry imbalance resulting from malfunction of the kidney excretory process. When waste products are retained, mental confusion increases in direct proportion to the buildup of the waste material.

He became dangerously combative in the ambulance. At the hospital, it took four of us to get him into bed. I briefed the attending physician on the patient's history. Afterward, we filed our mission reports and turned our medical gear in to the squadron.

Captain Armstrong picked me up the next morning. Since I had accumulated a lengthy "wish list" from Duong Duong, we headed for the PX to fill it. I completed my shopping and left for the hospital. Our patient's condition was critical. He had undergone surgery during the night and still was not improving. It was distressing news. We at Duong Duong had developed a special attachment to this young Army major

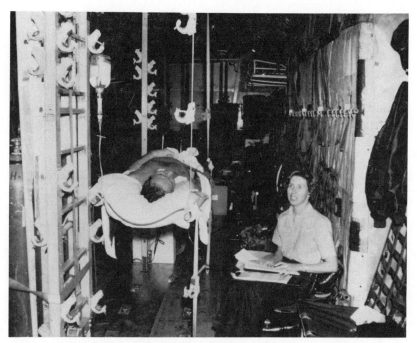

Capt. Virginia Armstrong attending to a medevac patient

when we had treated him months earlier. Now, despite everyone's best efforts, he was dying.

Before I returned to Saigon, there were many items that I needed to *cumshaw* from Clark's Central Supply Room. The CSR tech listened to my concerns and tolerated the lengthy list. We needed so many things, including surgical gloves. The tech handed me sixty pairs. There were a few other odds and ends—Ace bandages, nasal oxygen catheters, and Vaseline gauze—and I stuffed them all into a big cotton laundry bag I had brought.

From the CSR, I went to the Anesthesia Department. The senior anesthetist was sympathetic. Tweedie urgently needed Anectine, a muscle relaxant used for intubation (a procedure to insert a breathing tube between the vocal cords). I was given several vials.

The Orthopedic Brace Shop was the last stop. One of our corpsmen had injured himself severely in a recent Honda accident, sustaining a spinal-cord injury at neck level. A special neck brace would immobilize his head for the medevac flight. Duong Duong did not have the brace.

The Brace Shop tech, without hesitation, handed me exactly what I needed.

At 0600 the next morning, my return flight, on a C130A, departed. Because the C130A is primarily a cargo aircraft, there is no interior insulation to inhibit noise from the four, big turbo-prop engines. Earmufflike noise protectors were worn by the flight crews. Passengers were issued a wax earplug that molded itself to the ear canal shape. The early morning Luzon countryside was beautiful—just as I remembered it from the Korean War. Manila Bay, Corregidor, and the Bataan Peninsula appeared off the port wing. Within four hours, the plane descended over Tan Son Nhut.

The Viet Cong had set up a well-concealed heavy-caliber machine gun near the end of the main runway. Attempts to locate and destroy the gun had failed. As our C130A approached the runway, Viet Cong gunners began firing. Our pilot began a "high and hot" final approach.

The aircraft approached at a higher-than-normal altitude, then dropped rapidly onto the runway. I couldn't equalize the pressure in my right ear quickly enough. The pressure built until I suffered a blowout. There was a severe, sharp pain. Blood trickled into the ear canal. We landed and I stuck a tissue into my ear and left for the Ham Nghi.

The hospital received a call two days later: the major had died. We were deeply saddened. He had only ten days left on his Vietnam tour of duty. There was a military saying in Vietnam: "Nine days and a wake-up." On the tenth day, you woke up and flew out. It seemed that many personnel became casualties at the very end of their tours. We became superstitious. The tension kept us on edge during those last ten days.

Lt. Col. John C. Hughes was one of the most dedicated and interesting soldiers I met during my Vietnam tour. He was an Army helicopter pilot and the commanding officer of the 145th Aviation Battalion. Colonel Hughes came to Duong Duong frequently to check on his men. Because helicopters were such vulnerable aircraft, many of our casualties were chopper crew members. I got to know the colonel quite well. During one of the colonel's visits he said, "Since you girls take such good care of my boys, what can I do for you? How would you like to go for a Huey ride? I have a noncombat mission that I must make soon, so perhaps you and Tweedie would enjoy going along."

I had that Saturday off—the Fourth of July. At 0700, Tweedie and I arrived at the 145th's Flight Operations hut at Tan Son Nhut. The Huey waited on the flight line. I noticed an insignia painted on the door. It

Lt. Col. John Hughes and Corncob Six

was a pair of crossed yellow corncob pipes, with the numeral six between the crossed stems. The colonel arrived and told us the story behind the insignia and his radio-call sign, Corncob Six. Colonel Hughes
was an avid corncob pipe smoker; the six was the customary designa-
tion of command capacity.

The colonel's crew received a tip-off prior to each mission. If Hughes
arrived with a brown sock stuffed with tobacco and tied to his pistol
belt, the crew knew it would be a full day's mission. If the colonel arrived with an ordinary tobacco pouch, it meant a shorter day. That day,
a full brown sock swung from his belt.

Our flight plan called for stops at Phan Thiet, Da Lat, and Bao Lac,
and then back to Saigon. The U.S. and South Vietnamese forces jointly
used a tea plantation airstrip in Bao Lac for a staging area. The airstrip
needed a new windsock, which Colonel Hughes planned to deliver.

Tweedie and I donned flak jackets and climbed aboard Corncob Six.
We were joined by the colonel, his copilot, and two gunners. The
Huey's armament was impressive. There were two M-60 machine guns

on swivels at each door, four automatic rifles, and each man had a side arm buckled to his webbing. We also had two boxes of grenades and plenty of rounds of ammunition. Tweedie and I took jump seats directly aft of the pilots. We ascended immediately to 1500-feet altitude to avoid the possibility of attracting Viet Cong ground fire.

Phan Thiet's fog was disappearing as we approached the airstrip. I looked down on the tiny coastal village and saw a fishing fleet putting out to the South China Sea. We landed and saw an L-19 (a light reconnaissance aircraft) parked on the ramp. Capt. Paul Raetz, the pilot, was a former patient of ours. He was bound for Da Lat and offered to radio information concerning visibility. Forty-five minutes later, Paul called to say that the fog in the mountain passes was burning off.

We flew north to Da Lat. The town came into view, and we began a slow descent, landing at Cam Ly Military Air Base. All of us wanted to visit Madame Nhu's summer estate nearby. For ten piasters, visitors saw the picturesque grounds and the mansion's interior. The gates were locked. Tweedie and I were disappointed—we wanted at least to see Madame Nhu's $25,000 stainless-steel kitchen.

A few hours later, we landed in Bao Lac at the largest tea plantation in South Vietnam. Several thousand pounds of black tea leaves were harvested each day—tea fragrance filled the air. The plantation manager guided us on a tour of the facility, and when it was over I noticed dark clouds gathering in the distance. We hurried aboard Corncob Six, trying to avoid a monsoon.

The chopper headed south at dangerously low altitude, beneath a lowering ceiling of thick, angry clouds and sheets of rain. Suddenly, the mountaintops were above us as we maneuvered through the passes at cruising speed and only four hundred feet altitude above the north-south highway. We were well within range of Viet Cong ground fire. The door gunners armed their M-60s, and all hands kept watch below for evidence of bright orange muzzle flash.

We made it safely through the mountain passes. Clear weather and the coastal plains lay ahead. Corncob Six climbed to a safer altitude. But we were running low on fuel. Colonel Hughes announced an unscheduled stop at Bien Hoa Air Base for refueling.

At Bien Hoa, I hopped off the chopper for a look around. I wandered to a nearby hangar, where the doors were wide open. I couldn't believe my eyes. Two U-2 spy planes were parked inside. This was an exciting discovery. I examined one—half expecting to get thrown out of the hangar at any minute. But no one came in. I climbed on a wing and looked into the cockpit. There was instrumentation I recognized and some that I couldn't identify. I noticed the controls for the plane's cameras. I couldn't help thinking that someone should have locked those hangar doors. It was not common knowledge that U-2s were in Vietnam at the time.

Corncob Six touched down safely at Tan Son Nhut at 1700. Colonel Hughes and his men were ready for some rest; they were scheduled for a combat mission the next day. We arrived at the Ham Nghi and received bad news from Ann Richman. The major who commanded the Medevac "Dust Off" Unit had been killed earlier that day. While on a rescue mission in the Mekong Delta, his Huey had drawn hostile ground fire. The major was shot through the heart, the chopper crashed, and all hands were killed. Many times the major had checked in on the progress of casualties he had brought to Duong Duong. We all liked him and admired his innovative rescue techniques and his courage. The Fourth of July was not a safe day for a chopper mission after all.

Anyone familiar with the World War II China-Burma-India theater of operations remembers Gen. Joseph W. Stilwell—nicknamed Vinegar Joe. Vinegar Joe's son, Brig. Gen. Joseph W. Stilwell, Jr., commanded the U.S. Army Support Group, Vietnam. General Stilwell and I became good friends. Like Colonel Hughes, he often came to Duong Duong to visit the men he commanded. He inquired about their conditions, their needs, and presented many Air Medals and Purple Hearts. Often he arrived straight from the battlefield, still dressed in battle gear.

Cider Joe was a tough-fighting general who enjoyed flying helicopter gunship missions. He had several close calls and drew criticism when he exceeded the accepted risk factor. Gen. William Westmoreland had this to say of Cider Joe: "Young Joe was apparently never happier then when he was manning a machine gun in a helicopter, piloting a plane, or making free-fall parachute jumps. However adept he was at those jobs, they were hardly proper assignments for a senior officer who had other responsibilities."[*]

Cider Joe caught a flight aboard an outmoded Thai aircraft in 1966 and disappeared somewhere in the Pacific. The losses of General Stilwell and the other courageous pilots I knew during my Vietnam duty reminded me of the dangers wartime flight-line operations held. But in spite of inherent danger, there were also numerous achievements—and frequent acts of heroism.

[*]Gen. William C. Westmoreland, *A Soldier Reports* (New York: Dell, 1976), 74.

SEVENTEEN
Good-bye, Saigon

AUGUST 1964 saw General Westmoreland and the American forces confronting a disintegrating political situation. As for me, my tour of duty was winding down. It was a strange combination of violence and social niceties.

General Westmoreland had been unable to attend our anniversary tea, due to the visit of Secretary of Defense Robert McNamara. But he made up for it the second week in August, when the Westmorelands invited Duong Duong's senior nurses to dinner. The occasion was a visit by Colonel Mildred I. Clark, Director of the Army Nurse Corps.

For awhile that day, I didn't think we would make it to the general's dinner party. At 1150, as we were waiting behind Duong Duong for a ride to lunch, Saigon suddenly was rocked by a resounding blast. Several ambulances were dispatched to the downtown Caravelle Hotel. We stood by to receive casualties, but none arrived.

News of the Caravelle explosion did arrive. The Caravelle was the most popular hotel in Saigon. News correspondents occupied rooms on the fifth floor, which took the brunt of the blast. An investigation revealed that a heavy explosive charge had been placed in a room on the fifth floor; the blast nearly destroyed that floor and damaged two others. Fortunately, the journalists were not in their rooms at the time and Duong Duong received no casualties. Despite the damage and piles of shattered glass and debris, the human toll was not what it could have been.

We attended the dinner and met Colonel Clark and Lt. Gen. John L. Throckmorton, Westmoreland's new deputy. General Throckmorton was especially proud of his son, Army Capt. Thomas B. Throckmorton, also stationed in Vietnam.

We dined in an elegant room at the Westmorelands' villa at 60 Tran Qui Cap, near the Cercle Sportif. Later, the guests chatted and we got to know Colonel Clark quite well, inviting her to the Ham Nghi later that week. The dinner and setting were lovely, but in the distance we heard the muffled thunder of artillery fire. It continued throughout the evening.

Colonel Clark, who accepted our invitation, visited the Ham Nghi on what turned out to be a fairly exciting evening. From the balcony, we listened to artillery fire and watched the flare drops. Later, the colonel saw fifteen tanks pass along Ham Nghi Street below. Our group took the colonel to dinner at a nearby French restaurant, and when we stepped out on the street afterward, we were greeted by the scream of one of Duong Duong's ambulances. It careened around the corner and stopped in front of a building. We hurried over and watched as a man—an American civilian—was carried out. He was dead, the victim of a self-inflicted gunshot wound.

It was 13 August 1964. Duong Duong received a call from Tan Son Nhut's Flight Operations requesting an ambulance to pick up an incoming patient from Nha Trang. I accompanied the ambulance and arrived at Tan Son Nhut early. With time to kill, I took a seat on a nearby bench and watched the base activity. Tan Son Nhut in 1964 was the busiest airport in the world.

Things seemed fairly normal for a few minutes, until I noticed activity in the north sky. A line of olive-drab Hueys was approaching the base. They thundered overhead one after another, 110 choppers in all. I'd never witnessed anything like it.

An Air Force major joined me, and I asked him what was going on. He explained that the choppers were returning from Ben Cat, thirty miles to the north. The mission was to airlift two ARVN battalions to rout out a well-dug-in Viet Cong stronghold. I wondered if Duong Duong would receive casualties. Chopper crews and American advisers were involved in the mission. I returned to the hospital and waited. No casualties arrived from Ben Cat, but the afternoon ended with a bang.

I was in the ICU, facing windows that overlooked the Operating/Emergency Room area. Just as I inserted tubing into an IV (intravenous) bottle, there was an enormous explosion. The windows blew in, glass shattered, the IV tray crashed to the deck. Patients who could jumped from their beds and crouched under them.

For a few anxious moments I thought Duong Duong was under attack. My patients—soldiers straight from combat—thought so, too. We had all been on edge during August. An incident involving U.S. Navy ships in the Tonkin Gulf had occurred on 2 and 4 August; a state of national emergency had been declared on 8 August. All R and Rs had been canceled in case planes were needed to evacuate civilians. We were packed and ready to leave Saigon if so ordered. Because of the disintegrating situation, jet aircraft were ordered into Vietnam for recon and intercept missions.

No one in the ICU was hurt from the blast. There was no smoke or fire. I hurried to the Operating/Emergency Room area, the source of the main blast. There was no outside damage, no smoke, and no fire. But the inside was a mess! Windows were cracked, and an operating light in the ER fell from its overhead attachment, crashing and exploding onto the table. Luckily, no one was underneath at the time.

Tweedie and her corpsmen examined the smashed light. Since there wasn't evidence of an exploding bomb, I wondered what had caused the blast. I thought of the jets and the possibility of a sonic boom—my hunch was right. Minutes later, a call from General Westmoreland's office confirmed that a jet descending over the city had exceeded the sound barrier. A call went out to the squadron commander: no more sonic booms over Saigon.

A street mob scene that I was trapped in during June proved a prelude to virtual anarchy. There was looting, street fighting, killings, and mob rule. For Saigon, 27, 28, and 29 August became holocaust days.

Loudspeakers were installed in the park outside our quarters; the volume was at maximum level. Someone tried to whip the Vietnamese public into a frenzy, and the diatribes became so unbearable that I wanted to shoot holes through every speaker.

It was impossible to sleep. I was both physically and emotionally exhausted. Still, we managed to make our way to Duong Duong. The travel was hazardous, and I wasted no time returning to quarters. From our balcony, I saw many vicious, unbelievable atrocities. School children armed with nail-studded boards beat another child to death. Another time, I saw a boy drive a machete into another boy's abdomen, eviscerating the child, who stood for a moment clutching his intestines.

General Khanh stepped down. Martial law was instituted, and a curfew was put in effect. ARVN troops moved into Saigon, gradually restoring order.

At the very end of August, Tweedie and Walt received honors. The entire staff mustered in formation in the hospital compound one hot

Mob rule taking over the circle before Ham Nghi, 28 August 1964

morning. Capt. Archie Kuntz, Commanding Officer, HedSuppAct, read
the citations and pinned on the ribbons. They were honored with the
Secretary of the Navy Achievement Award. We nurses were extremely
proud of Tweedie. She worked long, difficult hours in her role as the
only staff anesthetist at Naval Station Hospital, Saigon.

My thirty-ninth birthday was on 31 August. I celebrated by doing
evening duty at Duong Duong. My Saigon tour was drawing to a close; I
had orders to the Naval Hospital, Portsmouth, Virginia. It wasn't quite
nine days and a wake-up—but it was close.

The last of the original seven Navy nurses stationed at the U.S. Naval
Station Hospital, Saigon, prepared to leave during September and October 1964. Of our pioneer group, only Jan Barcott had left prematurely
(having been medevaced to the States in December). Flo Alwyn and
Penny Kauffman, who originally had worked at the American Dispensary, had left Saigon during the spring. Tweedie Searcy received orders
to the Naval Hospital, Portsmouth, Virginia, and left 22 September. She
would be reorganizing the Navy's Nurse Anesthetist School of Anesthesia. Elaine King, Carleda Lorberg, and I were the last to go. Elaine
headed for the Naval Hospital, San Diego, California; Carleda had

Capt. Fisichella, surgeon Walt Zuckerman, Gen. William C. Westmoreland, the author, and Tweedie Searcy at a surprise farewell party

orders for Naval Hospital, Great Lakes, Illinois. Our plans were to depart
Saigon the second week of October.

It was a whirlwind of activities. On 3 September we went to Tan
Son Nhut to meet Tweedie's replacement and welcomed an old friend,
Comdr. Priscilla Miller. Pris moved into the Ham Nghi and began her
orientation. The pace quickened. Between hospital duties, we squeezed
in detachment preparations and a few farewell parties.

It was fortunate that during those final weeks, Duong Duong received no mass casualties. The daily hospital routine and Pris's indoctrination went smoothly. The never-ending drama viewed from our balcony impressed her. Flares continued to drop, artillery thundered, tracer

fire lighted the night skies. Civil unrest simmered; martial law was still in effect. We knew that at any moment, violence might erupt. Any new outbreak held the potential of closing the Tan Son Nhut Airport. And without airplanes, there wouldn't be any departures for home.

We chose the newly repaired Caravelle Hotel for Tweedie's 9 September farewell dinner. The lovely top-floor restuarant was back in service. Our guests included our surgeons, Drs. Walt Johnson, Walt Zuckerman, and Roy Smith; Priscilla Miller; and OR technicians.

I surveyed our banquet table, a smorgasbord of surgical and anesthesia talent. If a terrorist bomb exploded here, Duong Duong stood to lose most of its surgical staff. Just as I articulated this horrific thought, all hell broke loose. There was a brilliant flash followed by a loud crash. Window glass blew in, shattering, trapped by billowing drapes. An enormous vase crashed to the deck. Torrential monsoon rains swept into the room.

The Caravelle staff hurried to batten down the hatches. Our party jumped up, looked around, and decided that no one was hurt. Someone remarked that if I had any more hair-raising thoughts, I should just keep them to myself—*please!*

The second week of September, Stan Nakasone, one of Tweedie's OR techs, decided to surprise Tweedie, Walt Johnson, Walt Zuckerman, and me with a party, which was held on the hospital's fifth deck. He enlisted Kitsy Westmoreland to help. The Gray Ladies turned out too, and the goodies they provided were wonderful.

The highlight of the surprise party occurred when Generals Westmoreland and Throckmorton arrived. Both generals expressed gratitude for the care we gave their men. We were overcome that the commanding general and his deputy found a few minutes, despite enormous responsibilities, to visit us one last time. We were almost too overwhelmed to speak. The relationship between Army and Navy was indeed special. Providing the best possible medical care for American personnel in Vietnam was a cooperative and rewarding effort.

Finally, it *was* "nine days and a wake-up." The last letter to my parents was dated 1 October 1964. Replacements for Elaine and me arrived in country that day. My final hours were spent acclimating the newcomers to Duong Duong. It was a somewhat different Duong Duong than the one that I helped commission: the elevator was slightly more reliable, Central Supply had a roof, CSR corpsmen stayed cooler and drier, supplies accessed the pipeline more readily, and we *cumshawed* less.

On the downside, Miss Ninh's switchboard still blew fuses, terrified patients still rocketed across Tran Hung Dao Street to X-ray, bricks still filled traction buckets, and 105-mm howitzer shells still displayed gladioli.

There were many fine people I would miss at Duong Duong and elsewhere in Vietnam. There was a special fondness for the corpsmen— Paul Burns, Jim Manning, Stan Nakasone, and Joe Craney in particular. I held Walt Johnson in great esteem. Ann Richman, our chief nurse, would be greatly missed. Betty Murphy at the USO had become a great friend. The Vietnamese civilian staff, particularly Miss Ninh and Old Charley, were dear to me. So were the gentle Thai nurses.

I would miss the original seven. We were plank owners of "USS Duong Duong." For better or worse, the experience would never be duplicated. There were many "rocks and shoals," few gentle seas. We all completed our journey stronger, professionally enriched, and witnesses to the most compelling and dramatic world events of our time.

At the Ham Nghi, my duffel bags were packed. Thi Ba and Thi Hai, who had been brought in as a replacement for Thi Cong, were melancholy. I was very fond of these women. They were courteous, hardworking, and always willing to please. I'd miss their giggles, their charm, and their kindnesses. I knew I would never see them again.

The two-day checkout period was busy. I was debriefed and awarded the Vietnam Service Medal. On 9 October I officially detached from Headquarters Support Activity, Saigon.

That evening, two officers of the Special Forces, Maj. Donald Heibert and Maj. C. Hudlin, arrived at the Ham Nghi. They presented me with a wonderful gift that I cherish to this day. It is an elaborately hand-printed scroll in the colors of the Special Forces and the Rangers. It reads:

> Let it be known by these present that LCDR Bobbi Hovis by her professional competence and empathy for Special Forces Operational Detachments in the III Corps Tactical Zone has earned for herself the respect and admiration of Special Forces and is hereby awarded the title of "Green Bonnet."

I was taken by surprise at this gesture. I never learned how they found out that I was leaving, or whose idea the scroll was. The Special Forces are still favorites, with an exclusive place in my memories and my heart.

It was 10 October, "wake-up" day. Thi Ba and Thi Hai bid me a tearful good-bye. I left the Ham Nghi, leaving forever a front-row seat in rooms with a view of history in the making.

Carleda and Elaine were at Tan Son Nhut Airport when I arrived. It was sunny and hot, just like every other day. Our friends came for a final send-off—a few of the nurses, some corpsmen. There were hugs and tears.

Flight call was announced. I left the terminal and climbed the loading ramp. There was one last surprise. The World Airways 707 was the same plane that brought me to Vietnam one year earlier. And I was welcomed by one of the stewardesses who had been aboard that flight. I settled comfortably for the long flight home. We would arrive at Travis Air Force Base after stops in the Philippines, Guam, and Hawaii.

The engines started, and we rolled onto the taxi strip. I looked back at my friends and waved. We passed the main terminal, and the briefing hut, and aircraft, as far as I could see. Our ground speed increased, the nose lifted, we were off the deck. A gentle turn put us on course for Clark. The Vietnamese landmass slid from sight, and for the last time I headed over the deep blue South China Sea. These were the final moments of my Vietnam tour. Good-bye, Saigon.

Epilogue

ON 1 DECEMBER, I began my tour as supervisor of the ICU at U.S. Naval Hospital, Portsmouth, Virginia. It was an adjustment. The hospital was enormous, with a staff of hundreds. Dozens of corpsmen and young nurses received training in the ICU. It seemed that I almost never had a free moment. Still I was experiencing Vietnam in so many ways.

Letters from friends in Vietnam arrived regularly. It was always enjoyable to hear from the staff at Duong Duong in particular. Our Vietnam casualty load increased daily at Portsmouth: our staff attrited fifty or sixty people at a time. Most of these people shipped to Vietnam, often assigned to the hospital ships *Repose* and *Sanctuary*. Later, Lt. Cmdr. Charlotte Clark, a nurse anesthetist, received orders to U.S. Naval Station Hospital, Saigon.

Lt. Ruth Purinton, my assistant, received a Vietnam assignment and wrote of events in Da Nang. Comdr. Bill Mahaffey, an anesthesiologist, shipped out to a field hospital near the DMZ. His many letters were informative.

One letter asked me to watch for a young Marine medevaced to Portsmouth. Bill had administered anesthesia to the patient. As he recovered after surgery, he persistently requested a chocolate malted milkshake—which Bill promised. A few days later, I found the young Marine. He couldn't believe it when I walked in carrying a chocolate milkshake.

Pris Miller, Tweedie's replacement, was the most prolific writer. Her letters updated me on all the Duong Duong activities. Duong Duong's improvement campaign continued. More storage was added and improvements to Central Supply were completed. The elevator continued to resist all efforts at repair. And Pris kept me updated on life at the Ham Nghi—Thi Ba and Thi Hai were fine.

On Christmas Eve 1964, Viet Cong terrorists drove a jeep loaded with a 300-pound bomb into the Brink BOQ, blowing it up. Three months later, terrorists used several hundred pounds of *plastique* explosives to destroy the U.S. Embassy in Saigon. Pris wrote of the devastation: two Americans and eleven Vietnamese were killed. Many were wounded, including Deputy Ambassador U. Alexis Johnson. Even the My Canh floating restaurant, an American favorite, was blown up twice. Saigon was still Bombsville.

Walt Johnson left the Navy and established a successful surgical practice in Taunton, Massachusetts. Tweedie Searcy continued running the School of Anesthesia at Portsmouth until her retirement in 1968. She now resides in Annapolis, Maryland. The remaining members of the original seven are retired or left the Navy. I hear occasionally from Jan Barcott through the Navy Nurse Corps Association newsletter; I've not heard from the others.

In doing research for this book, I found that information about U.S. Naval Station Hospital, Saigon, was almost nonexistent. There was, for example, no record of staff present for the hospital's commissioning. The few bits of information I did find came primarily from Frank Uhlig, Jr.'s, book *Vietnam: The Naval Story.*

U.S. Naval Station Hospital, Saigon, was transferred to the U.S. Army in March 1966. In twenty-nine months of Navy operation, Duong Duong hospitalized more than 6,000 patients. There were also in excess of 130,000 outpatients treated. Victims of terrorist activities and battle casualties treated at the hospital were not recorded until 1 November 1964.

An archivist I consulted found so little information that to me it was as though the hospital had never existed. But it did, and despite the apparent lack of historical record, U.S. Naval Station Hospital, Saigon, existed as a significant chapter in the annals of Navy medicine and the Navy Nurse Corps.

Bibliography

Baker, Mark. *Nam*. New York: William Morrow, 1981.
Bamford, James. *The Puzzle Palace*. New York: Penguin, 1983.
Browne, Malcomb W. *The New Face of War*. New York: Bobs Merrill, 1965.
Burdick, Eugene. *Sarkan*. New York: Putnam, 1966.
Cady, John F. *Southeast Asia—Its Historic Development*. New York: McGraw-Hill, 1964.
Clark, Wallace and Anne. *Army and Navy Nurses in World War II*. New York: Military Nurse Publishing Co. (no date).
Claude, Edmond. *Vietnam, Past and Present*. Vietnam Department of National Education, 1957.
Department of Defense. *A Pocket Guide to Viet-Nam*. Washington, D.C.: U.S. Government Printing Office, 1962.
Depauw, Linda Grant. *Seafaring Women*. Boston: Houghton Mifflin, 1982.
Doan Bich and Le Trang. *Saigon in the Flesh*.
Do Van Minh. *Vietnam, Where East and West Meet*. Milan, Italy: Amilcare, Pizzi (no date).
Downs, Hunton. *The Compassionate Tiger*. New York: Putnam, 1960.
Duncan, Donald. *The New Legions*. New York: Pocketbooks, 1967.
Fall, Bernard B. *Hell in a Very Small Place*. Philadelphia: Lippincott, 1966.
Fall, Bernard B. *Street Without Joy*. Harrisburg, Pa.: Stackpole, 1966.
Fall, Bernard B. *Two Vietnams: A Political and Military Analysis*, 2nd rev. ed. New York: Praeger, 1967.
Furgurson, Ernest B. *Westmoreland: The Inevitable General*. Boston: Little, Brown, 1968.
Gettleman, Marvin E. *Vietnam*. New York: Fawcett, 1965.
Greene, Graham. *The Quiet American*. New York: Viking, 1956.
Grey, Anthony. *Saigon*. New York: Dell, 1983.

BIBLIOGRAPHY

Halberstam, David. *The Making of a Quagmire.* New York: Random House, 1965.
Halberstam, David. *The Best and the Brightest.* New York: Random House, 1969.
Halberstam, David. *The Powers That Be.* New York: Dell, 1980.
Harvey, Frank. *Air War—Vietnam.* New York: Bantam, 1967.
Hauptley, Denis J. *In Vietnam.* New York: Atheneum, 1985.
Higgins, Marguerite. *Our Vietnam Nightmare.* New York: Harper & Row, 1965.
Just, Ward. *To What End.* Boston: Houghton, 1968.
Just, Ward. *Military Men.* New York: Knopf, 1970.
Larteguy, Jean. *The Centurians.* Paris: Presses de la Cité, 1960.
Larteguy, Jean. *The Praetorians.* New York: Dutton, 1963.
Larteguy, Jean. *Yellow Fever.* New York: Avon, 1967.
Lawson, Don. *An Album of the Vietnam War.* New York: Franklin Watts, 1986.
Lederer, William, and Eugene Burdick. *The Ugly American.* New York: Norton, 1958.
Mangold, Tom, and John Penycate. *The Tunnels of Cu Chi.* New York: Berkley Books, 1986.
Mecklin, John. *Mission in Torment.* New York: Doubleday, 1965.
Meiring, Desmond. *The Brinkman.* Boston: Houghton, 1964.
Monigold, Glenn W. *Folk Tales of Vietnam.* New York: The Peter Pauper Press, 1964.
Moore, Robin. *The Green Berets.* New York: Crown, 1965.
Moore, Robin. *The Country Team.* New York: Crown, 1967.
Nav. Med. 939. *The White Task Force.* Washington, D.C.: U.S. Government Printing Office, 1945.
Nav. Pers. *The White Task Force.* Washington, D.C.: U.S. Government Printing Office, 1949.
Rigg, Col. Robert B. *How To Stay Alive in Vietnam.* Harrisburg, Pa.: Stackpole, 1966.
Roy, Jules. *The Battle of Dien Bien Phu.* R. Julliard, 1963.
Shaplen, Robert. *The Lost Revolution: United States in Vietnam. 1946–1966.* New York: Harper & Row, 1965.
Smith, S.E. *The United States Navy in World War II.* New York: Ballantine, 1967.
Snepp, Frank. *Decent Interval.* New York: Vintage Press, 1978.
Thayer, Charles W. *Guerilla.* New York: Signet, 1965.
Tregaskis, Richard W. *Vietnam Diary.* New York: Popular Library, 1966.
Uhlig, Frank, Jr. *Vietnam, The Naval Story.* Annapolis, Md.: Naval Institute Press, 1986.
Warner, Denis. *The Last Confucian.* Baltimore: Penguin Books, 1964.
West, Morris L. *The Ambassador.* New York: Morrow, 1965.

Westmoreland, General William C. and Admiral U.S.G. Sharp. *Report on the War in Vietnam.* Washington, D.C.: U.S. Government Printing Office, 1969.

Westmoreland, General William C. *A Soldier Reports.* New York: Dell, 1976.

Wolfestone, Daniel. *The Golden Guide to South and Southeast Asia.* Hong Kong: Far Eastern Economic Review.

Index

About the Author

LCDR Hovis was commissioned into the Navy Nurse Corps in 1947 after graduating from the Western Pennsylvania Hospital School of Nursing, Pittsburgh, Pennsylvania. An ensign of twenty-three who had not yet owned a car, she earned her pilot's license and purchased a Piper J3 aircraft while stationed in Key West, Florida. In 1950 she completed Air University Flight Training, becoming a Designated Navy Flight Nurse.

She participated in the Korean Airlift in 1950–51, serving with the 1453 Medical Air Evacuation Squadron. Hovis was the first Navy nurse to volunteer for Vietnam; she served from September 1963 to October 1964 at U.S. Navy Station Hospital, Saigon—the first U.S. Navy hospital in South Vietnam. For her service in the U.S. Navy Nurse Corps, she was awarded seven medals and decorations.

Hovis retired in 1967 to Annapolis, Maryland, where she maintains close ties with the U.S. Naval Academy through its sailing, football, and basketball programs. She was a sailing instructor for the Naval Academy Sailing Squadron, of which she was the first female member.